EASY PIANO

SIMPLE CHRISTMAS SONGS

THE EASIEST EASY PIANO SONGS

ISBN 978-1-4950-9722-5

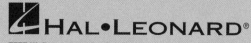

7777 W. BLUEMOUND RD. P.O. BOX 13819 MILWAUKEE, WI 53213

Visit Hal Leonard Online at
www.halleonard.com

ALL I WANT FOR CHRISTMAS IS MY TWO FRONT TEETH

Words and Music by
DON GARDNER

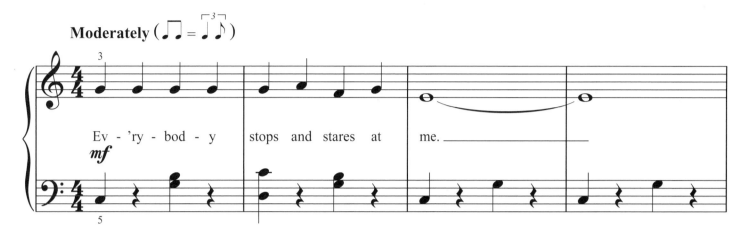

Ev - 'ry - bod - y stops and stares at me. _____

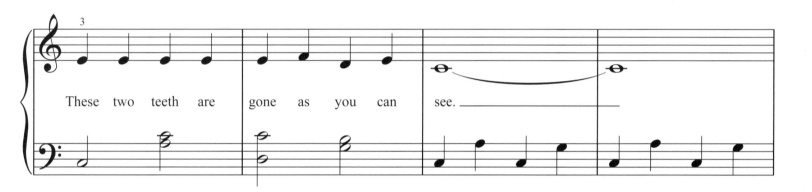

These two teeth are gone as you can see. _____

I don't know just who to blame for this ca - tas - tro - phe! But

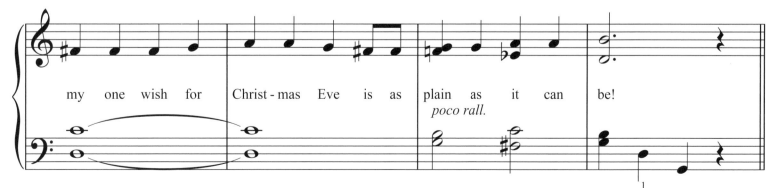

my one wish for Christ - mas Eve is as plain as it can be!

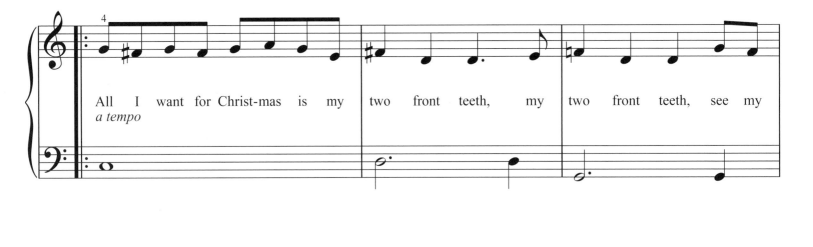

All I want for Christ-mas is my two front teeth, my two front teeth, see my

a tempo

two front teeth! Gee, if I could on-ly have my two front teeth, then

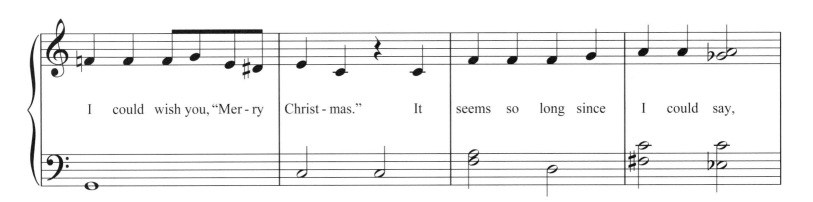

I could wish you, "Mer-ry Christ-mas." It seems so long since I could say,

"Sis-ter Su-sie sit-ting on a this-tle!" Gosh, oh gee, how hap-py I'd be, if

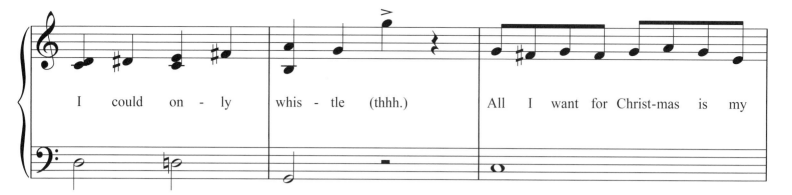

I could on - ly whis - tle (thhh.) All I want for Christ-mas is my

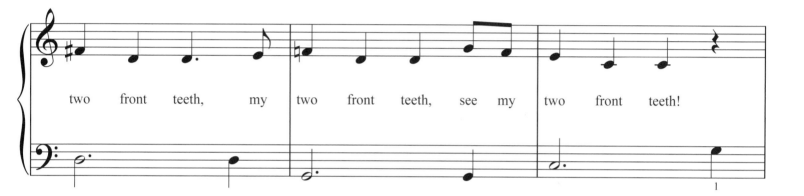

two front teeth, my two front teeth, see my two front teeth!

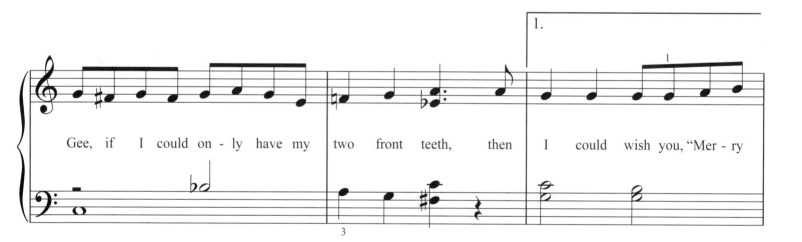

Gee, if I could on - ly have my two front teeth, then I could wish you, "Mer - ry

Christ - mas!" I could wish you "Mer - ry Christ - mas!"

All I WANT FOR CHRISTMAS IS YOU

Words and Music by MARIAH CAREY
and WALTER AFANASIEFF

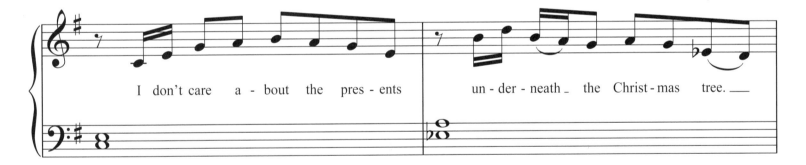

Make my wish come true: ___ all I ___ want for Christ-mas is you. ___

Moderately (♩♩ = ♩♪³)

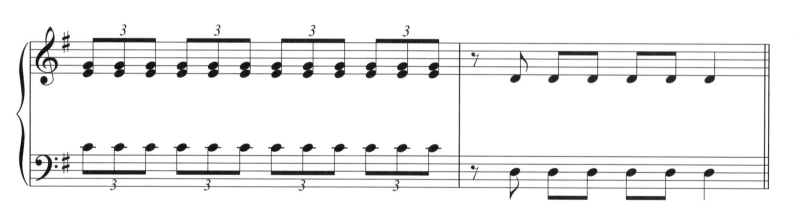

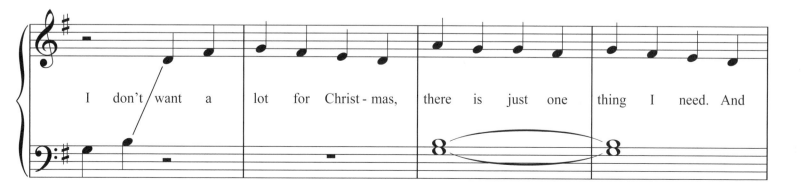

I don't want a lot for Christ-mas, there is just one thing I need. And

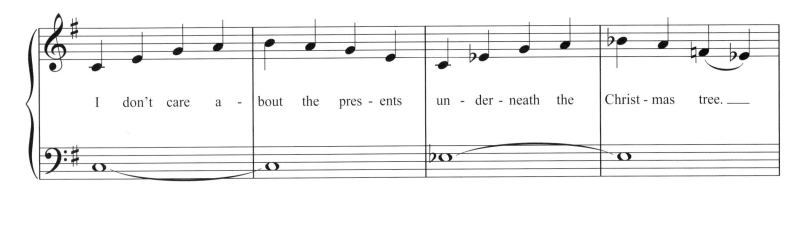

I don't care a - bout the pres - ents un - der - neath the Christ - mas tree. ___

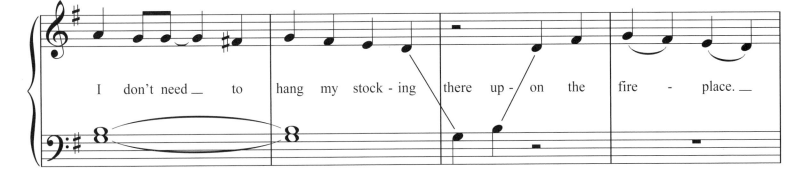

I don't need ___ to hang my stock - ing there up - on the fire - place. ___

San - ta Claus won't make me hap - py with a toy on Christ - mas day. ___

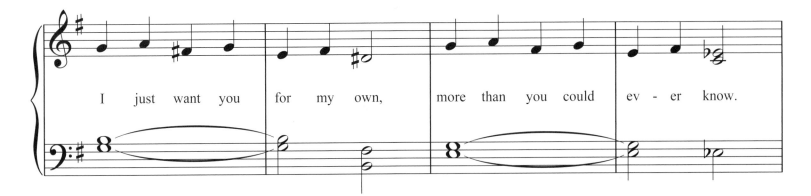

I just want you for my own, more than you could ev - er know.

Make my wish come true. ____ Ba - by, all I want for Christ - mas ____

____ is ____ you. ____

Oo, ____ ba - by. ____ All I want for Christ - mas is

you, ____ ba - by. ____ ba - by. ____

BABY, IT'S COLD OUTSIDE
from the Motion Picture NEPTUNE'S DAUGHTER

By FRANK LOESSER

Female: I

real - ly can't stay. ___
sim - ply must go. ___
Male: But ba - by, it's cold ___ out - side. ___
Male: But ba - by, it's cold ___ out - side. ___

I've got to go 'way. ___
The an - swer is "no!" ___
But ba - by, it's
But ba - by, it's

cold out - side. ___
cold out - side. ___

This eve - ning has been ___
The wel - come has been ___
Been hop - ing that you'd drop in. ___
How luck - y that you dropped in. ___

so ___ ver - y
so ___ nice and

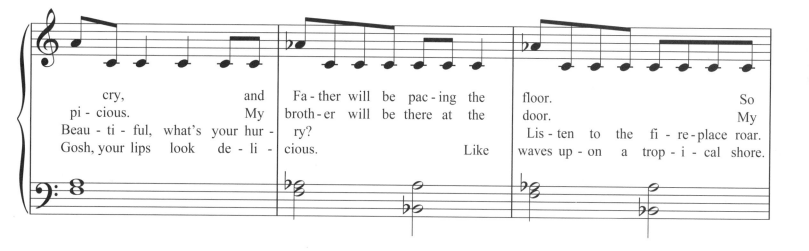

My neigh-bors might think. _
I've got to get home.
Ba - by, it's bad out there!
Ba - by, you'd freeze out there. _

Say!

(Spoken:) Say, darling,

Put some rec-ords on while I pour.
Nev - er such a bliz-zard be - fore.

What's in this drink?
can you lend me your comb?
No cabs to be _ had out there. _
It's up to your _ knees out there. _

I wish I knew how _
You've real - ly been grand, _

Your eyes are
I thrill when

to _ break the spell.
but _ don't you see?
like star - light _ now
you touch my _ hand.
I'll take your hat.
How can you do

Your hair looks swell.
this thing to me?

I
There's

ought to say, "No,   no,   no, sir!"   At
bound to   be   talk   to -   mor-row.   At
                              Mind if   I   move   in
                              Think of   my   life - long

least I'm gon-na say ___ that   I   tried.
least there will be plen - ty im - plied.
clos - er?
sor - row

                    I   real - ly   can't   stay.
                    I   real - ly   can't   stay.
What's the sense   of hurt - ing my pride?   Oh   ba - by, don't hold
if   you caught pneu-mo - nia and died.   Get   o - ver that old

out.   *Both:* Ah,   but   it's
doubt.

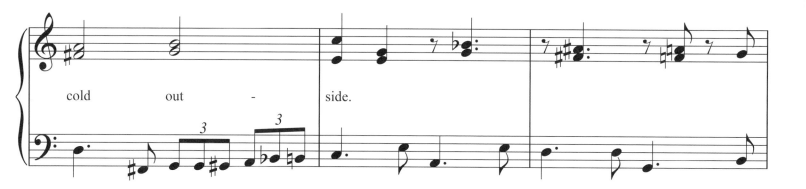

cold   out -   side.

1.

Female: I

2.

BELIEVE

from Warner Bros. Pictures' THE POLAR EXPRESS

Words and Music by GLEN BALLARD
and ALAN SILVESTRI

Moderately slow

Chil - dren sleep - ing, snow is soft - ly
Trains move quick - ly to their jour - ney's

fall - ing. Dreams are call - ing
end. Des - ti - na - tions

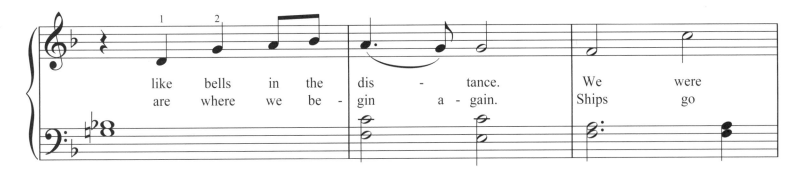

like bells in the dis - tance. We were
are where we be - gin a - gain. Ships go

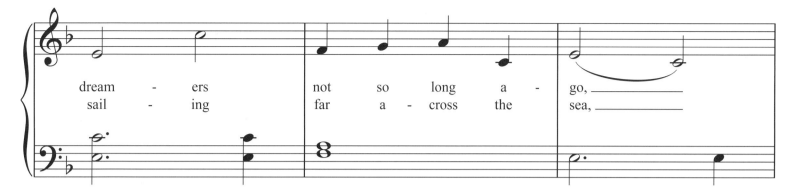

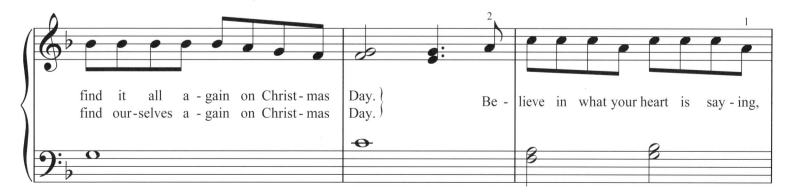

hear the mel - o - dy that's play - ing. There's no time to waste, there's so much to cel - e - brate. Be -

lieve in what you feel in - side and give your dreams the wings to fly.

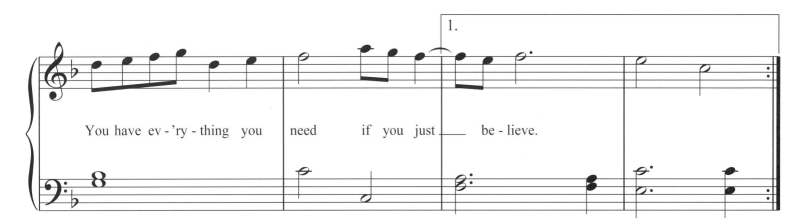

1.

You have ev - 'ry - thing you need if you just ___ be - lieve.

2.

___ be - lieve. *rit.*

CAROLING, CAROLING

Words by WIHLA HUTSON
Music by ALFRED BURT

With a lilt

Car - ol - ing, car - ol - ing, now we go; Christ - mas bells are ring - ing!
Car - ol - ing, car - ol - ing, thru the town; Christ - mas bells are ring - ing!
Car - ol - ing, car - ol - ing, near and far; Christ - mas bells are ring - ing!

mf

Car - ol - ing, car - ol - ing thru the snow; Christ - mas bells are ring - ing!
Car - ol - ing, car - ol - ing up and down; Christ - mas bells are ring - ing!
Fol - low - ing, fol - low - ing yon - der star; Christ - mas bells are ring - ing!

Joy - ous voic - es sweet and clear; sing the sad of heart to cheer.)
Mark ye well the song we sing; glad - some tid - ings now we bring.
Sing we all this hap - py morn; lo, the King of Heav'n is born.)

Ding, dong, ding, dong, Christ - mas bells are ring - ing!

BLUE CHRISTMAS

Words and Music by BILLY HAYES
and JAY JOHNSON

Moderately, in 2

I'll have a blue Christ - mas with - out you; _____

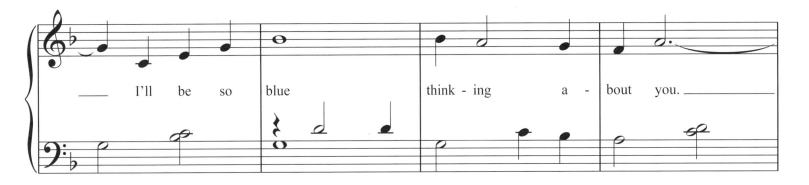

_____ I'll be so blue think - ing a - bout you. _____

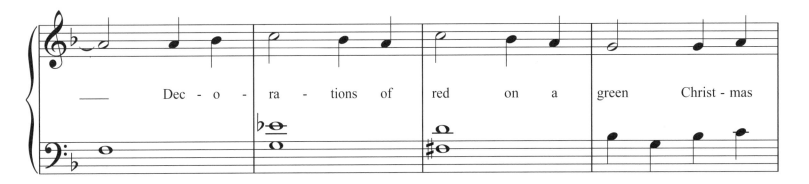

_____ Dec - o - ra - tions of red on a green Christ - mas

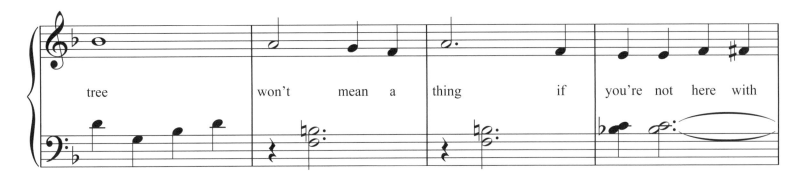

tree won't mean a thing if you're not here with

me. I'll have a blue   Christ - mas,   that's   cer - tain; _____

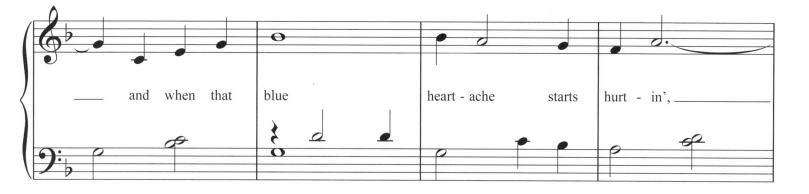

_____ and when that blue   heart - ache   starts   hurt - in', _____

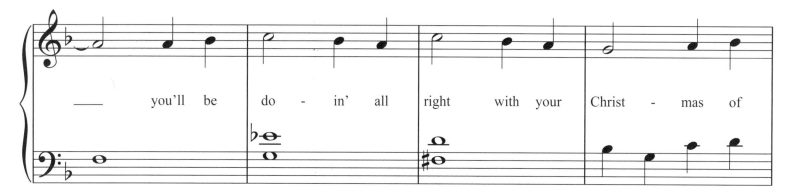

_____ you'll be   do - in' all   right   with your   Christ - mas of

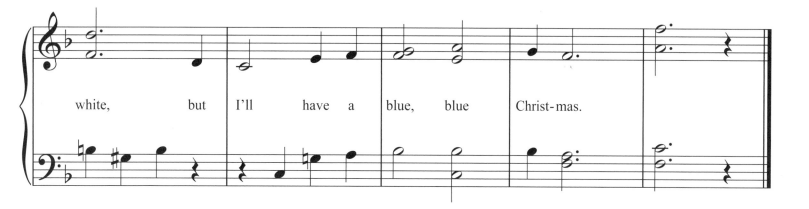

white,   but   I'll   have a   blue, blue   Christ-mas.

A CHILD IS BORN

Music by THAD JONES
Lyrics by ALEC WILDER

Slow Jazz Ballad

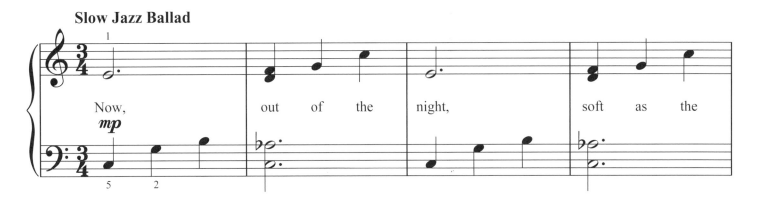

Now, out of the night, soft as the

dawn, in - to the light. This

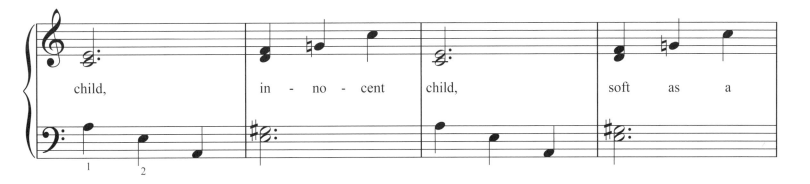

child, in - no - cent child, soft as a

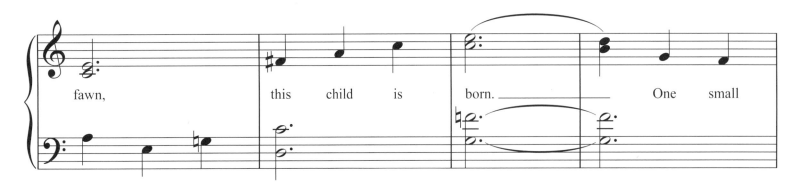

fawn, this child is born. _____ One small

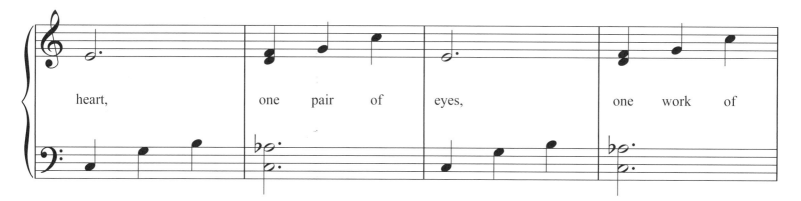

heart,   one   pair   of   eyes,   one   work   of

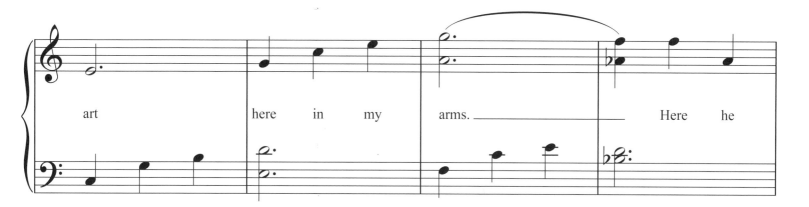

art   here   in   my   arms.   Here   he

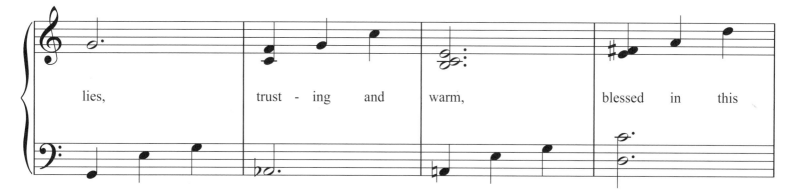

lies,   trust - ing   and   warm,   blessed   in   this

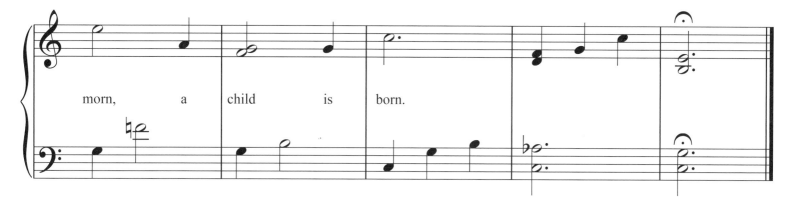

morn,   a   child   is   born.

THE CHIPMUNK SONG

Words and Music by
ROSS BAGDASARIAN

Happily

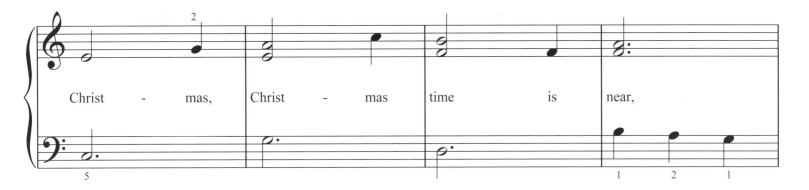

Christ - mas, Christ - mas time is near,

time for toys and time for cheer.

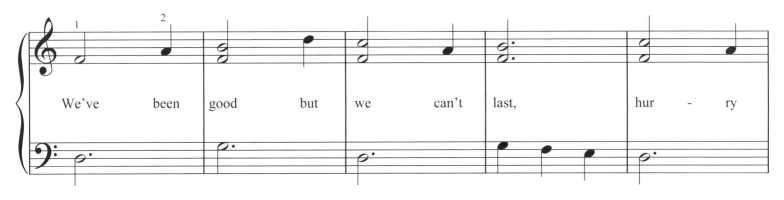

We've been good but we can't last, hur - ry

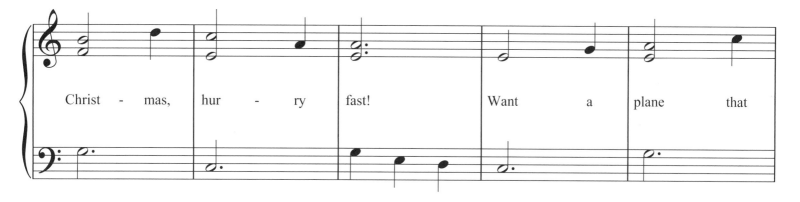

Christ - mas, hur - ry fast! Want a plane that

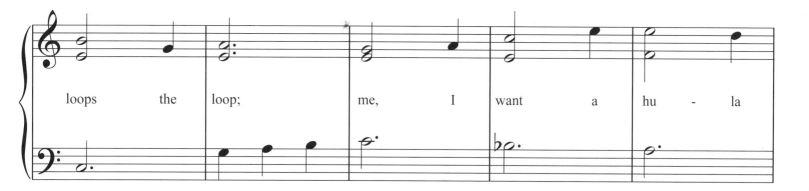

loops the loop; me, I want a hu - la

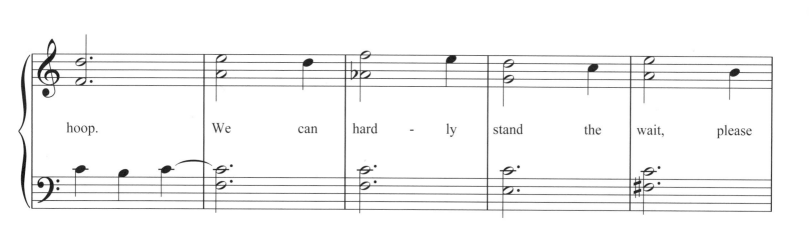

hoop. We can hard - ly stand the wait, please

Christ - mas, don't be late. _____

2

THE CHRISTMAS SONG
(Chestnuts Roasting on an Open Fire)

Music and Lyric by MEL TORMÉ
and ROBERT WELLS

Chest-nuts roast-ing on an o-pen fire, Jack Frost nip-ping at your

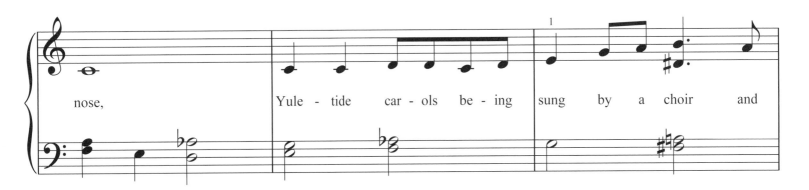

nose, Yule-tide car-ols be-ing sung by a choir and

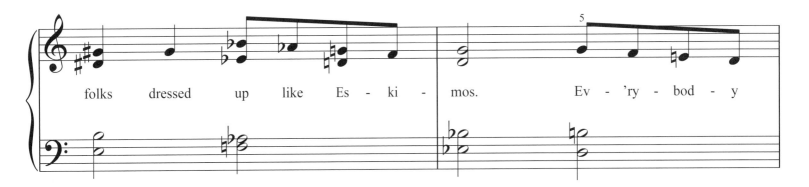

folks dressed up like Es-ki-mos. Ev-'ry-bod-y

knows a tur-key and some mis-tle-toe help to make the sea-son

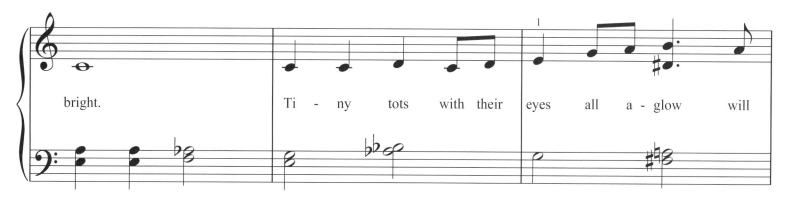

bright.　　　　　Ti - ny tots with their eyes all a - glow will

find it hard to sleep to - night.　　They know that San - ta's on his

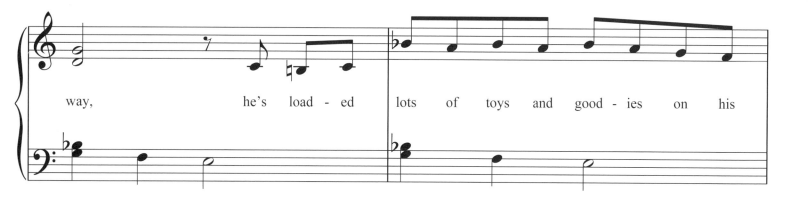

way,　　　　he's load - ed lots of toys and good - ies on his

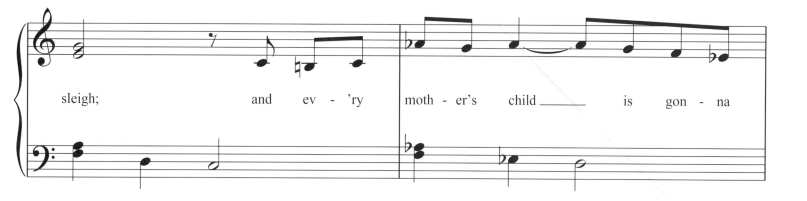

sleigh;　　　　and ev - 'ry moth - er's child ____ is gon - na

spy _____ to see if rein - deer real - ly know how to

fly. And so, I'm of - fer - ing this sim - ple phrase to

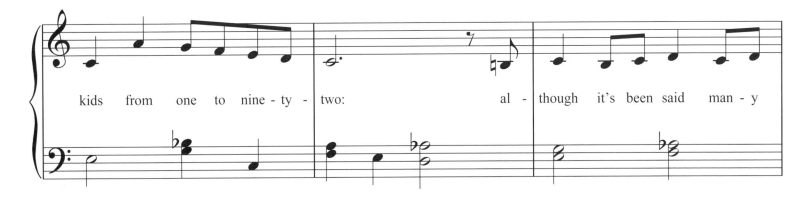

kids from one to nine - ty - two: al - though it's been said man - y

times, man - y ways, Mer - ry Christ - mas to you.

rit.

CHRISTMAS TIME IS HERE
from A CHARLIE BROWN CHRISTMAS

Words by LEE MENDELSON
Music by VINCE GUARALDI

Slowly

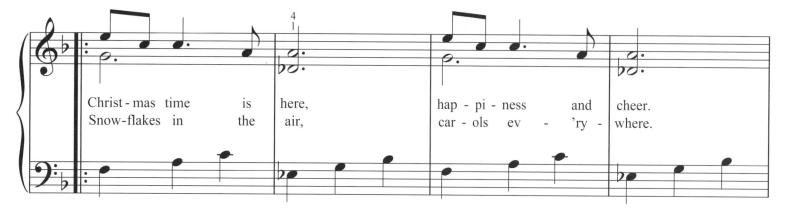

Christ - mas time is here, hap - pi - ness and cheer.
Snow - flakes in the air, car - ols ev - 'ry - where.

Fun for all that chil - dren call their fa - v'rite time of year.
Old - en times and an - cient rhymes of love and dreams to

share.　　　　　　　Sleigh - bells　in　the　air,

beau - ty　ev - 'ry - where.　　　　Yule - tide　by　the

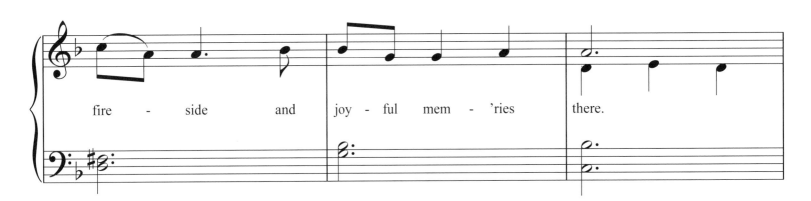

fire - side　and　joy - ful　mem - 'ries　there.

Christ-mas time　is　here,　we'll be draw - ing　near.

To Coda

Oh, that we could al - ways see such spir - it through the

year. *Instrumental*

1.

2.

D.S. al Coda

Instrumental ends

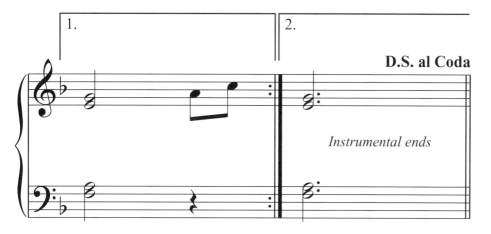

CODA

year.

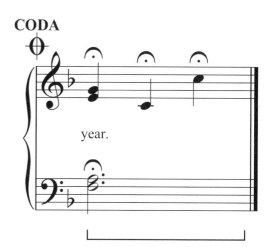

CHRISTMAS WRAPPING

Words and Music by
CHRIS BUTLER

Fast

Bah, hum - bug! No, that's too strong 'cause it is my fa - v'rite

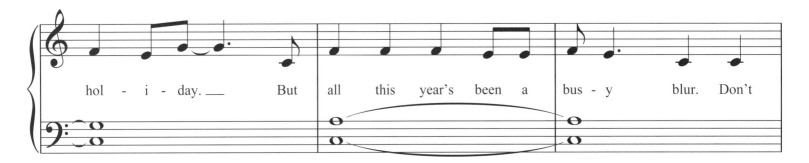

hol - i - day. ___ But all this year's been a bus - y blur. Don't

think I have the en - er - gy to add to my ___ al -

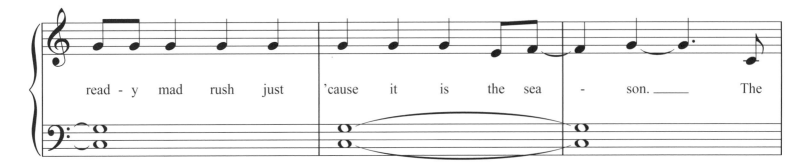

read - y mad rush just 'cause it is the sea - son. ___ The

per - fect gift for me would be _____ com - ple - tions and con - nec -

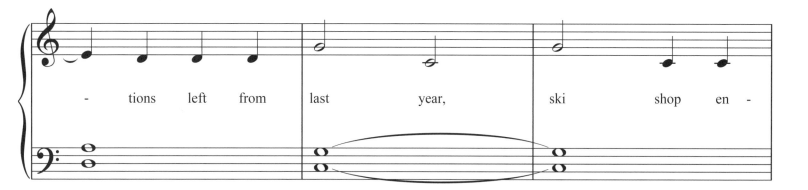

- tions left from last year, ski shop en -

coun - ter, most in - t'rest - ing. _____ Had his num - ber, but

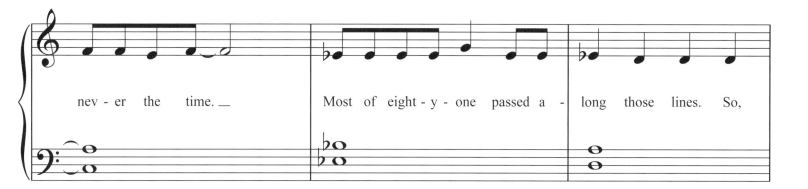

nev - er the time. _____ Most of eight - y - one passed a - long those lines. So,

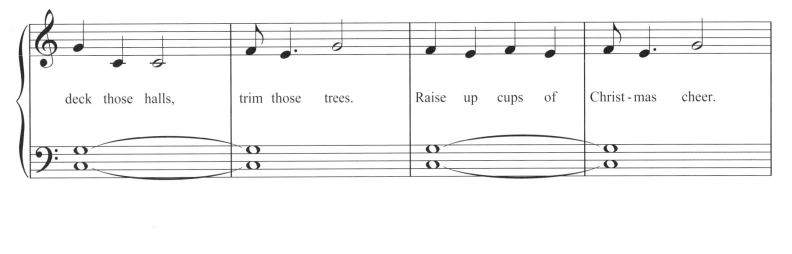

deck those halls,   trim those trees.   Raise up cups of   Christ-mas cheer.

I just need to catch my breath.   Christ-mas by my-self this year.

Cal-en-dar pic - ture,

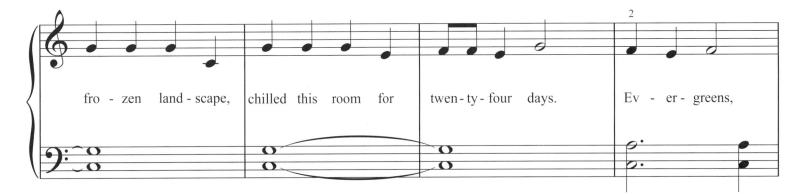

fro - zen land-scape,   chilled this room for   twen-ty-four days.   Ev - er - greens,

spar - kl - ing snow, get this win - ter o - ver with! Flash - back to spring - time,

saw him a - gain. __ Would - 've been good to go for lunch. Could - n't a - gree we're

both free. We tried, we said we'd keep in touch. Did - n't, of course, till

sum - mer - time, __ out to the beach to his boat, could I join him? No, this time

it was me. ___ Sun- burn in the third de - gree. ___ Now the cal - en- dar's

just one page, of course I am ex - cit - ed. ___ To - night's the night, ___ I

set my mind not to do too much a - bout ___ it.

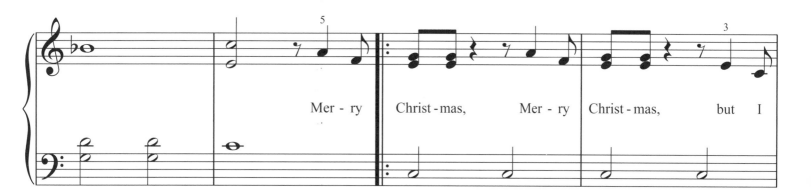

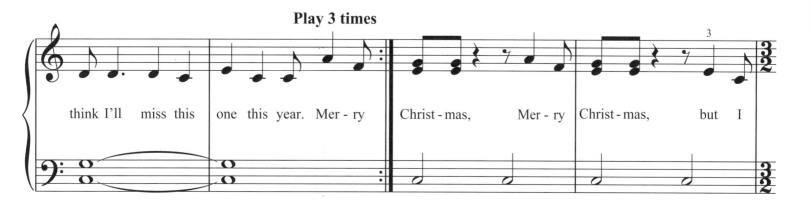

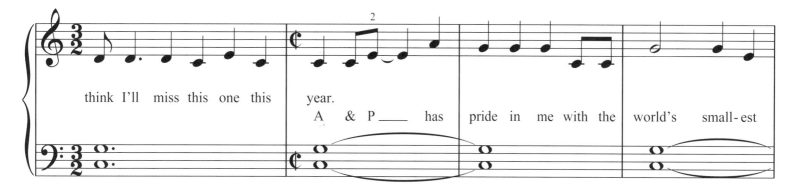

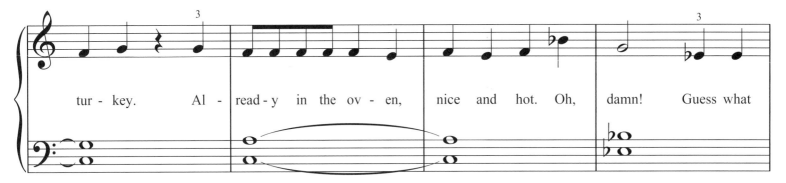

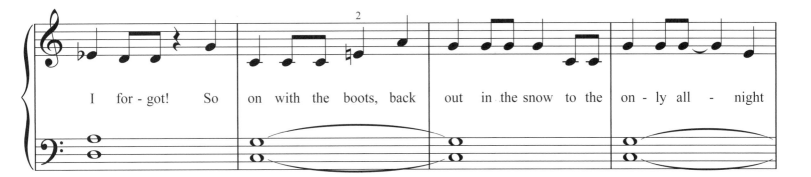

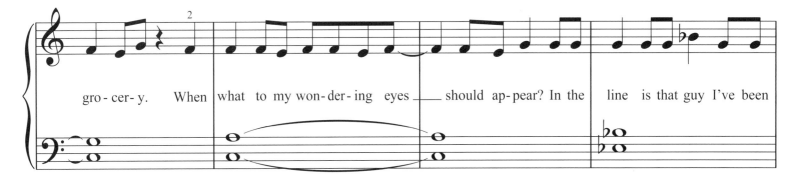

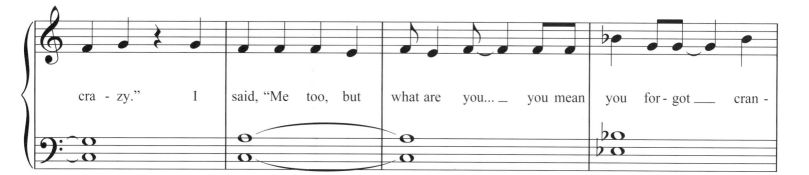

cra - zy."   I   said, "Me   too, but   what are   you...   you mean   you for - got   cran -

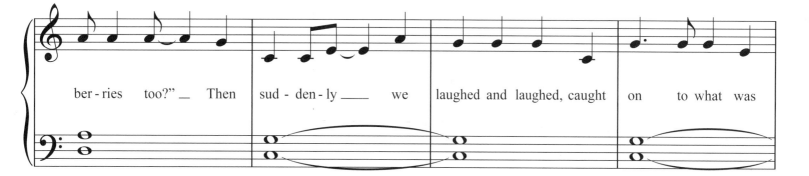

ber - ries   too?"   Then   sud - den - ly   we   laughed and laughed, caught   on   to what was

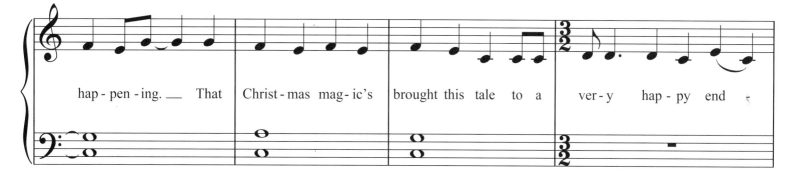

hap - pen - ing.   That   Christ - mas mag - ic's   brought this tale   to   a   ver - y   hap - py   end

ing.

DO THEY KNOW IT'S CHRISTMAS?
(Feed the World)

Words and Music by BOB GELDOF
and MIDGE URE

Moderate Rock

But say a prayer to pray for the oth - er ones

at Christ - mas time. It's hard, but when you're hav - ing fun, __

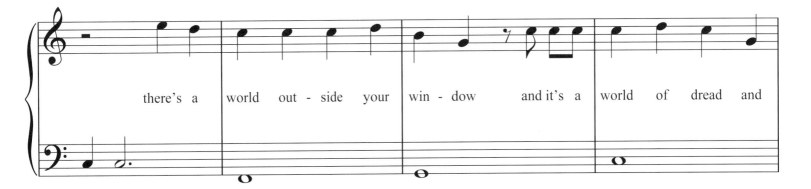

there's a world out - side your win - dow and it's a world of dread and

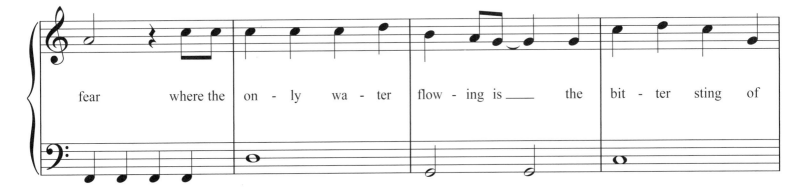

fear where the on - ly wa - ter flow - ing is __ the bit - ter sting of

tears.　　And the　Christ - mas　bells ＿　that　ring ＿ there　　　are the　clang - ing　chimes　of

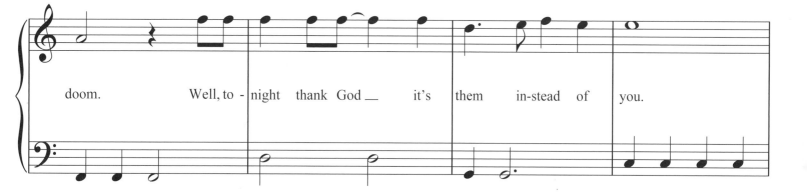

doom.　　　Well, to - night　thank God ＿　it's　them　in-stead　of　you.

And there　won't　be　snow ＿　in　Af - ri - ca ＿＿　this　Christ - mas　time. ＿

The　great - est　gift ＿＿　they'll　get　this　year ＿　is　life.

Do they know it's Christ - mas time at all?

Feed the world, _____ let them know it's
gain.

Christ - mas time a - Christ - mas time a - gain.

DO YOU HEAR WHAT I HEAR

Words and Music by NOEL REGNEY
and GLORIA SHAYNE

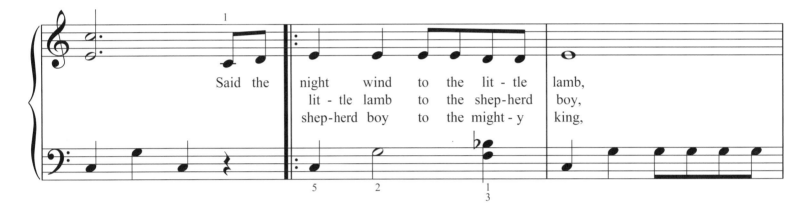

Said the | night wind to the lit - tle | lamb,
lit - tle lamb to the shep-herd | boy,
shep-herd boy to the might - y | king,

"Do you see what I see, _____
"Do you hear what I hear, _____
"Do you know what I know, _____

'way up in the sky, lit - tle
ring - ing through the sky, shep-herd
in your pal - ace warm, might - y

lamb?
boy?
king?

Do you see what I see? _____
Do you hear what I hear? _____
Do you know what I know? _____

A
A
A

star, a star, danc - ing in the night, with a tail as big as a
song, a song, high a - bove the tree, with a voice as big as the
Child, a Child shiv - ers in the cold; let us bring Him sil - ver and

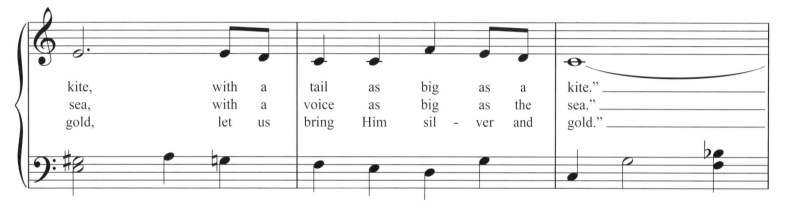

kite, with a tail as big as a kite." _____
sea, with a voice as big as the sea." _____
gold, let us bring Him sil - ver and gold." _____

1., 2.

3.

_____ Said the _____ Said the king to the peo - ple ev - 'ry
_____ Said the

where, "Lis - ten to what I say: _____

Pray for peace, peo - ple ev - 'ry - where! Lis - ten to what I say: __

__ The Child, the Child sleep - ing in the night, He will

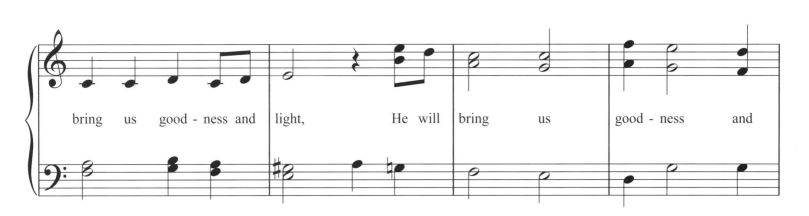

bring us good - ness and light, He will bring us good - ness and

light! *rall.*

HAVE YOURSELF A MERRY LITTLE CHRISTMAS

from MEET ME IN ST. LOUIS

Words and Music by HUGH MARTIN
and RALPH BLANE

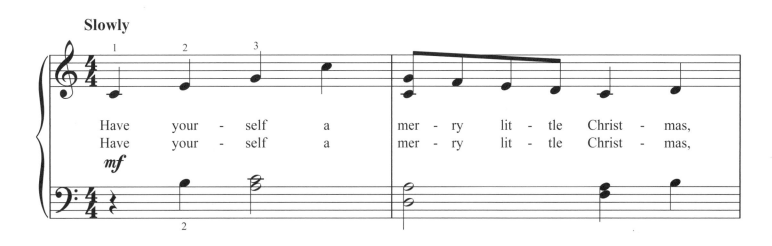

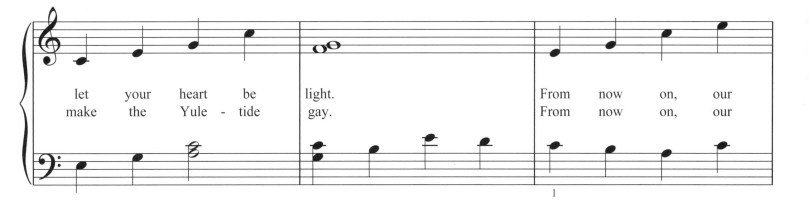

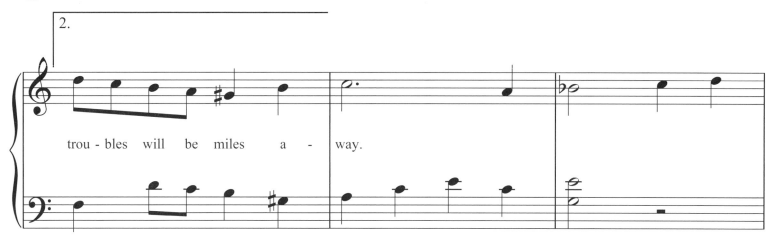

trou - bles will be miles a - way.

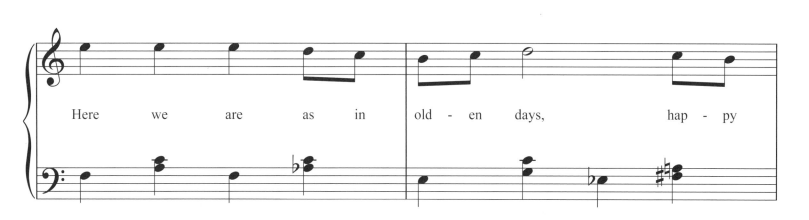

Here we are as in old - en days, hap - py

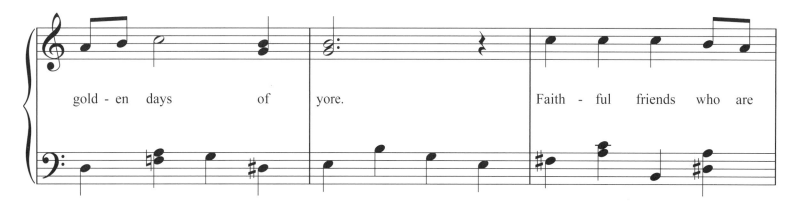

gold - en days of yore. Faith - ful friends who are

dear to us gath - er near to us once more.

Through the years we all will be to - geth - er, if the Fates al -

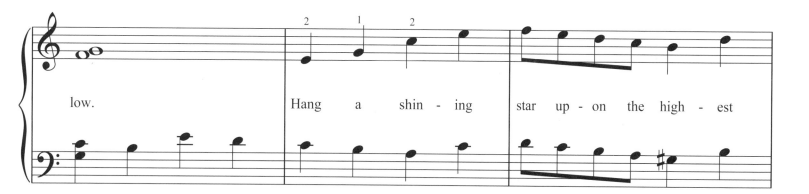

low. Hang a shin - ing star up - on the high - est

bough, and have your - self a

mer - ry lit - tle Christ - mas now. *rit.*

FELIZ NAVIDAD

Music and Lyrics by
JOSÉ FELICIANO

Moderately

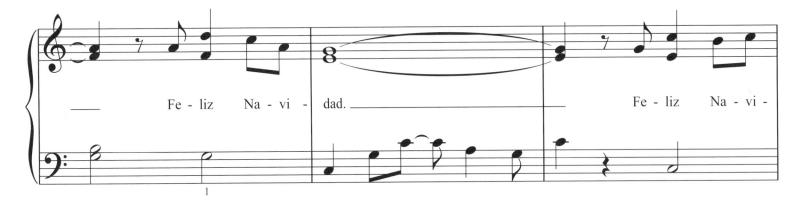

dad. Pros - pe - ro   a - ño y fe - li - ci - dad.

___ Fe - liz Na - vi - ___   I want to wish you   a

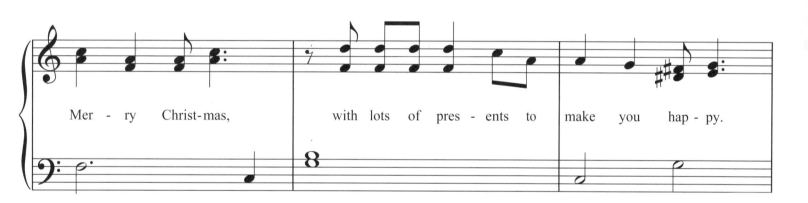

Mer - ry Christ-mas,   with lots of pres - ents to make you hap - py.

I want to wish you a   Mer - ry Christ-mas from the   bot - tom of my

52

heart. _____ I want to wish you a Mer - ry Christ-mas

with mis - tle - toe and __ lots of cheer, _ with lots of laugh-ter through-

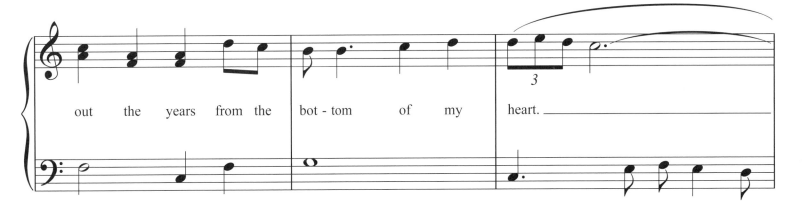

out the years from the bot - tom of my heart. _____

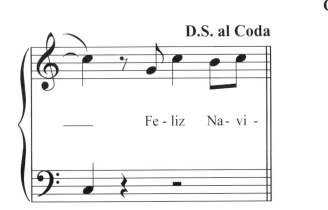

D.S. al Coda

_____ Fe - liz Na - vi -

CODA

A HOLLY JOLLY CHRISTMAS

Music and Lyrics by
JOHNNY MARKS

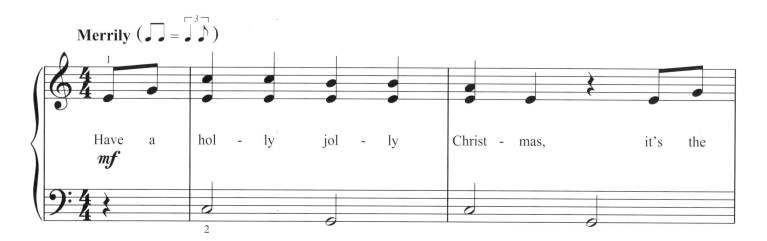

Have a hol - ly jol - ly Christ - mas, it's the

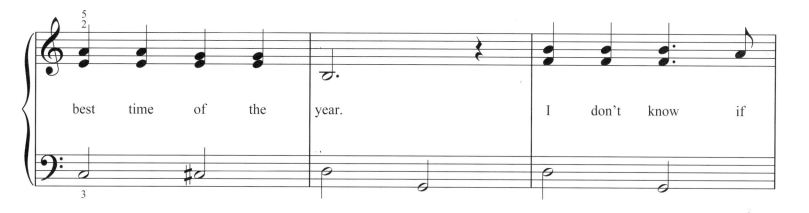

best time of the year. I don't know if

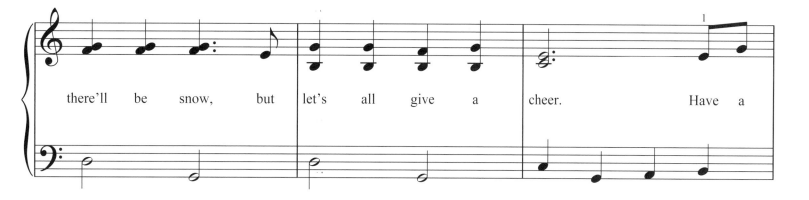

there'll be snow, but let's all give a cheer. Have a

hol - ly jol - ly Christ - mas and when you walk down the

street, say hel - lo to friends you know and

ev - 'ry - one you meet. Oh, ho, the

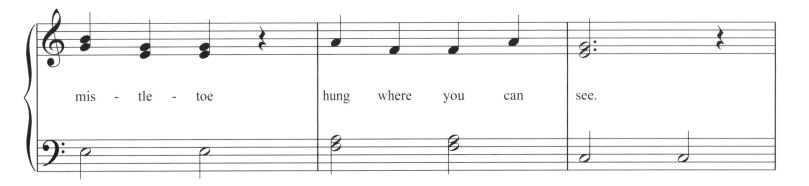

mis - tle - toe hung where you can see.

Some - bod - y waits for you, kiss her once for

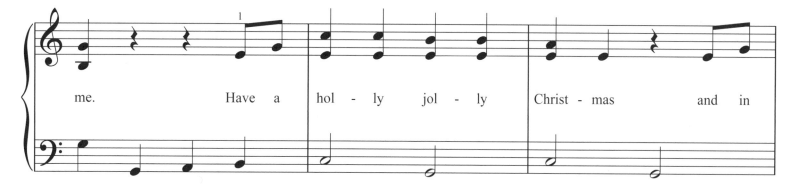

me. Have a hol - ly jol - ly Christ - mas and in

case you did - n't hear, oh by gol - ly, have a

hol - ly jol - ly Christ - mas this year.

FROSTY THE SNOW MAN

Words and Music by STEVE NELSON
and JACK ROLLINS

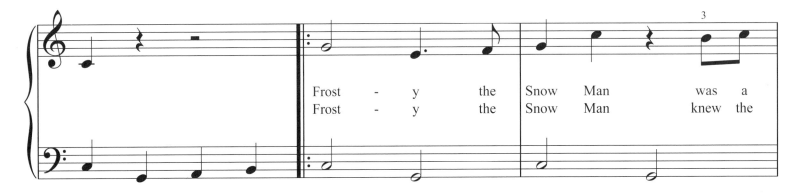

Frost - y the Snow Man was a
Frost - y the Snow Man knew the

jol - ly hap - py soul, with a corn - cob pipe and a
sun was hot that day. So he said, "Let's run and we'll

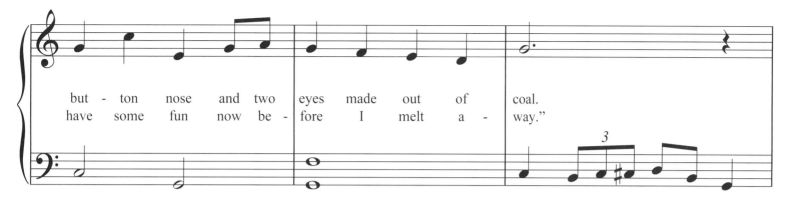

but - ton nose and two eyes made out of coal.
have some fun now be - fore I melt a - way."

Frost - y the Snow Man is a fair - y tale they
Down to the vil - lage with a broom - stick in his

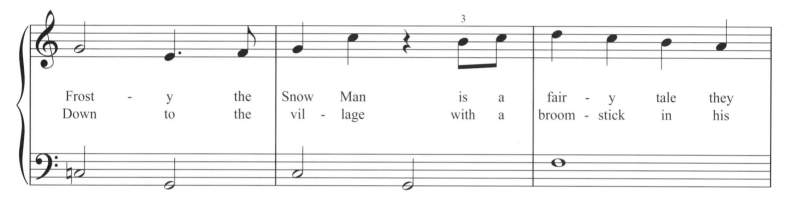

say; he was made of snow, but the chil - dren know how he
hand, run - ning here and there all a - round the square, say - in',

came to life one day. There must have been some
"Catch me if you can." He led them down the

mag - ic in that old silk hat they found, for
streets of town to the left and to the right. He

when they placed it on his head, he be - gan to dance a -
ran so fast he dis - ap - peared, yep, he was out of

round. Oh, Frost - y the Snow Man was a -
sight. Oh, For Frost - y the Snow Man had to

live as he could be, and the chil - dren say he could
hur - ry on his way, but he waved good - bye, say - in',

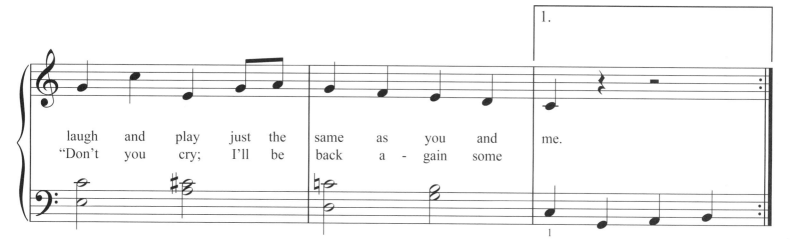

laugh and play just the same as you and me.
"Don't you cry; I'll be back a - gain some

day." Thump-e - ty thump thump, thump-e - ty thump thump,

look at Frost - y go! Thump-e - ty thump thump,

thump-e - ty thump thump, o - ver the hills of snow!

GRANDMA GOT RUN OVER
BY A REINDEER

Words and Music by
RANDY BROOKS

Grand-ma got run o-ver by a rein-deer

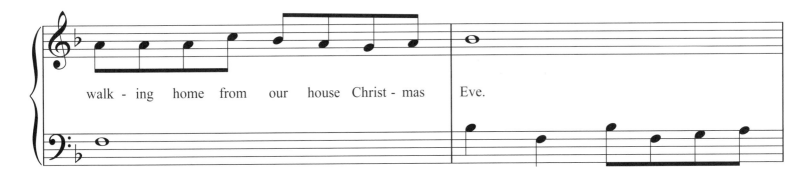

walk-ing home from our house Christ-mas Eve.

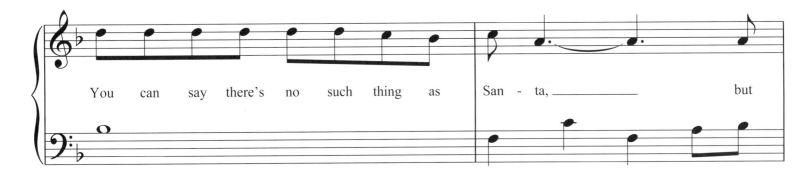

You can say there's no such thing as San-ta, but

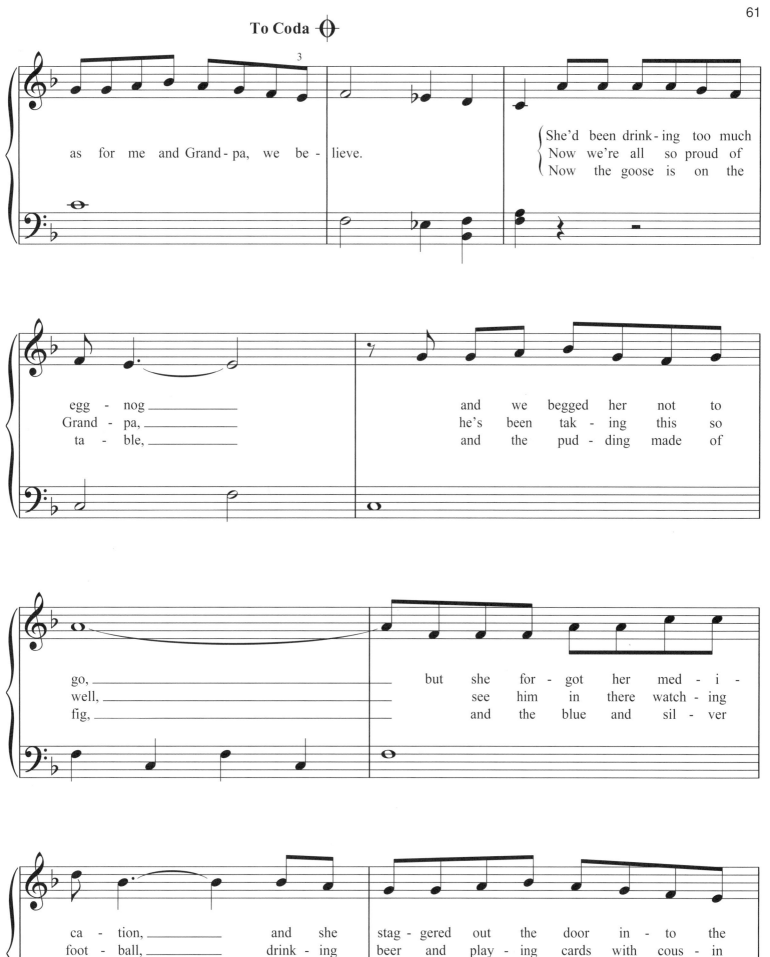

To Coda

as for me and Grand - pa, we be - lieve.

She'd been drink - ing too much
Now we're all so proud of
Now the goose is on the

egg - nog
Grand - pa,
ta - ble,

and we begged her not to
he's been tak - ing this so
and the pud - ding made of

go,
well,
fig,

but she for - got her med - i -
see him in there watch - ing
and the blue and sil - ver

ca - tion, and she
foot - ball, drink - ing
can - dles that would

stag - gered out the door in - to the
beer and play - ing cards with cous - in
just have matched the hair in Grand - ma's

snow.
Mel.
wig.

When we found her Christ - mas
It's not Christ - mas with - out
I've warned all my friends and

morn - ing
Grand - ma.
neigh - bors,

at the scene of the at -
All the fam - 'ly's dressed in
bet - ter watch out for your -

tack,
black,
selves.

she had hoof - prints on her
and we just can't help but
They should nev - er give a

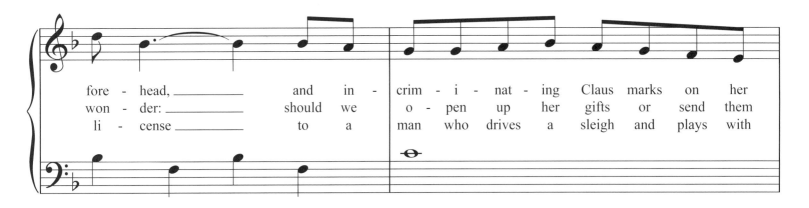

fore - head,
won - der:
li - cense

and in -
should we
to a

crim - i - nat - ing Claus marks on her
o - pen up her gifts or send them
man who drives a sleigh and plays with

Grand-ma got run o-ver by a rein-deer _____ walk-ing home from our house Christ-mas

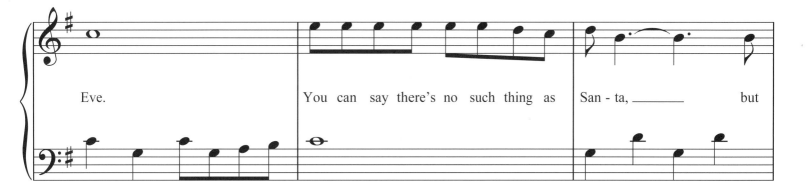

Eve. You can say there's no such thing as San-ta, _____ but

as for me and Grand-pa, we be-lieve. _____

back.
back?   elves.

D.S. al Coda

CODA
lieve.

HAPPY XMAS
(War Is Over)

Written by JOHN LENNON
and YOKO ONO

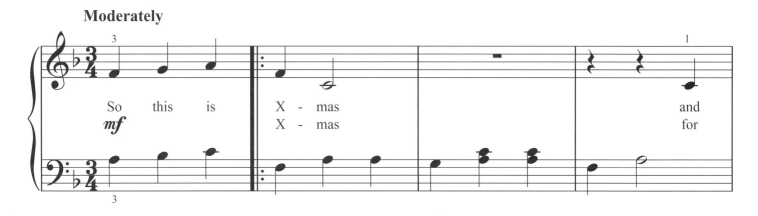

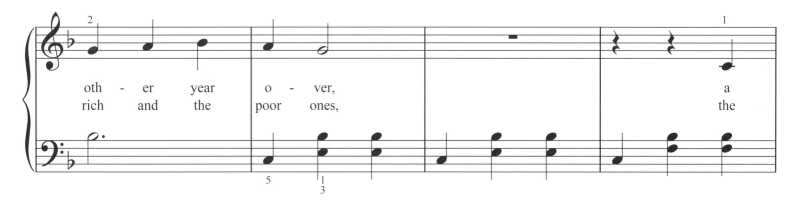

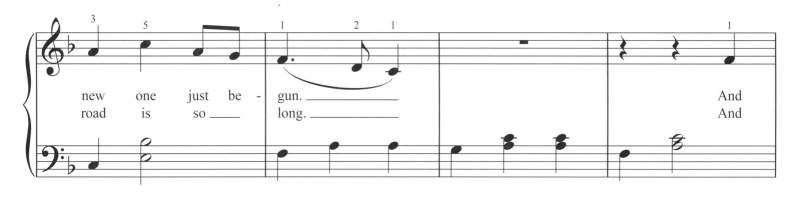

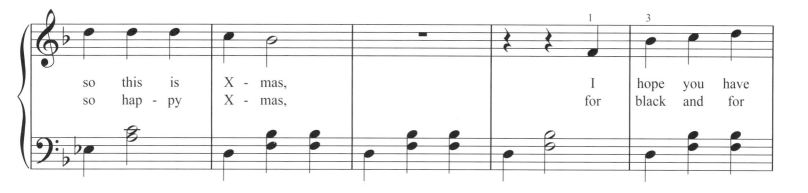

so this is X - mas,
so hap - py X - mas,
I hope you have
for black and for

fun,
white,
the near and the
for the yel - low and

dear ones,
red ones,
the old and the
let's stop all the

young. _____
fights. _____
A mer - ry, mer - ry

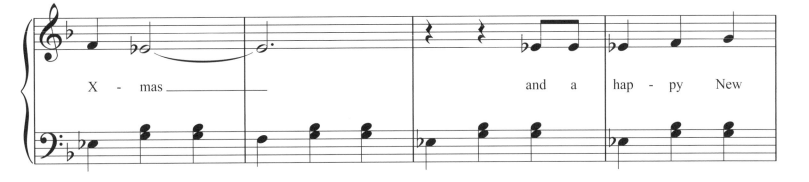

X - mas _____ and a hap - py New

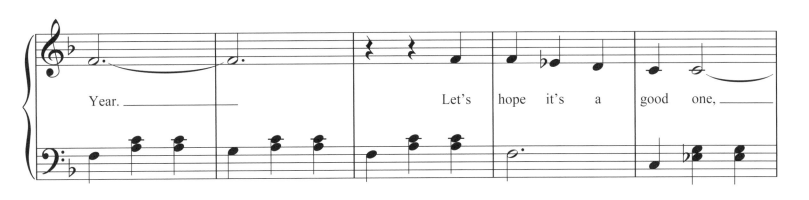

Year. _____ Let's hope it's a good one, _____

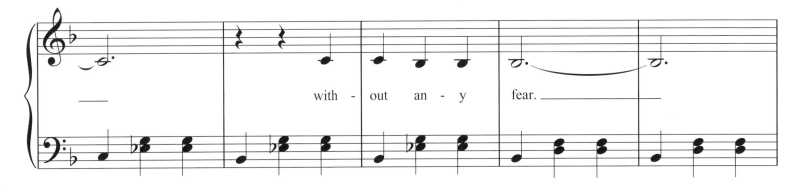

_____ with - out an - y fear. _____

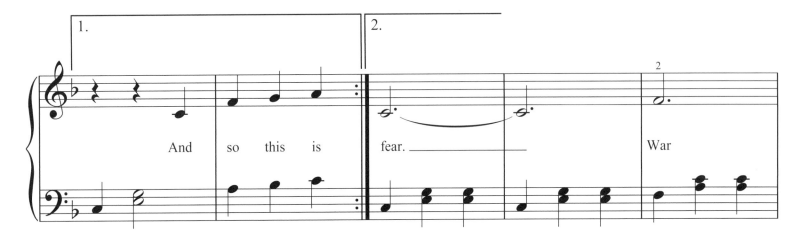

1.

And so this is

2.

fear. _____ War

is o - ver if you

want it. War is o -

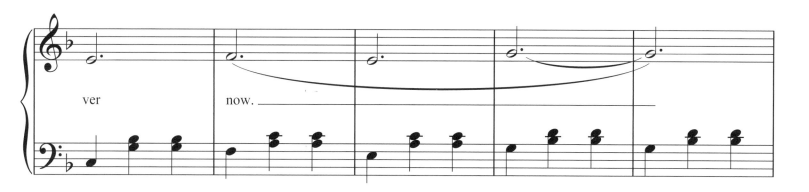

ver now.

p   *rit.*

HERE COMES SANTA CLAUS

(Right Down Santa Claus Lane)

Words and Music by GENE AUTRY
and OAKLEY HALDEMAN

Moderately bright

Bells are ring - ing, children sing - ing, all is mer - ry and
Hear those sleigh - bells jin - gle jan - gle, what a beau - ti - ful
San - ta knows that we're God's chil - dren, that makes ev - 'ry - thing
Peace on earth will come to all if we just fol - low the

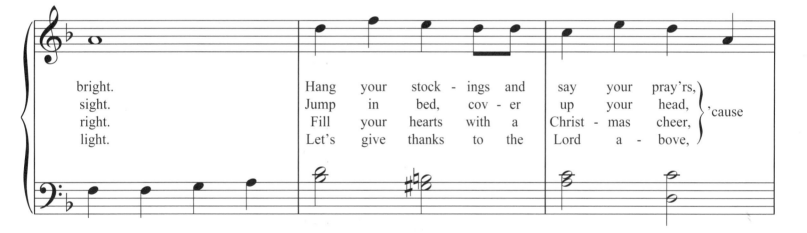

bright.
sight.
right.
light.

Hang your stock - ings and say your pray'rs,
Jump in bed, cov - er up your head,
Fill your hearts with a Christ - mas cheer, } 'cause
Let's give thanks to the Lord a - bove,

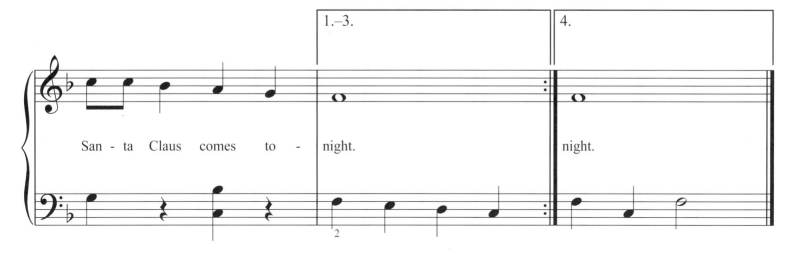

1.–3.

San - ta Claus comes to - night.

4.

night.

JINGLE BELL ROCK

Words and Music by JOE BEAL
and JIM BOOTHE

now the jin - gle hop has be - gun. ___ in the frost - y

air. What a bright time, ___ it's the right time ___ to

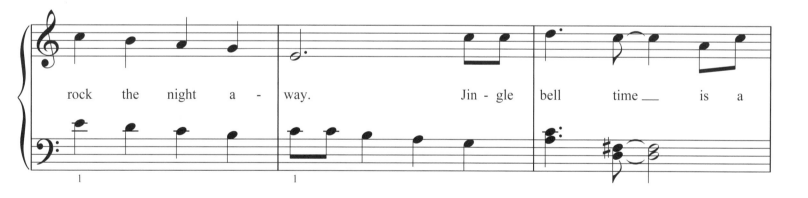

rock the night a - way. Jin - gle bell time ___ is a

swell time ___ to go glid - in' in a one-horse sleigh. _

Gid - dy - ap, jin - gle horse, pick up your feet, ___

jin - gle a - round the clock. Mix and min - gle in a

jin - gl - in' beat, ___ that's the jin - gle bell, that's the jin - gle bell,

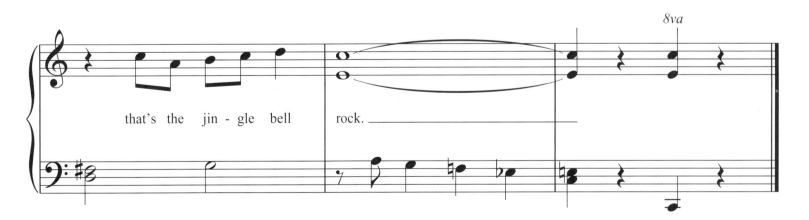

that's the jin - gle bell rock. ___

I HEARD THE BELLS ON CHRISTMAS DAY

Words by HENRY WADSWORTH LONGFELLOW
Adapted by JOHNNY MARKS
Music by JOHNNY MARKS

Moderately

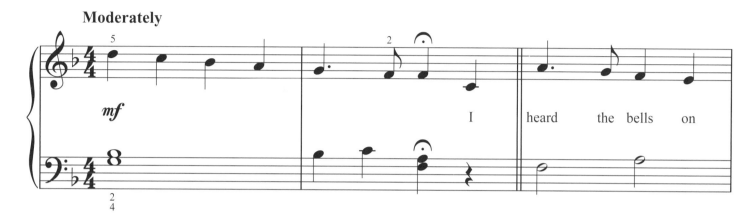

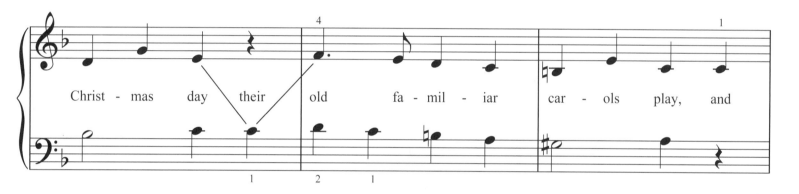

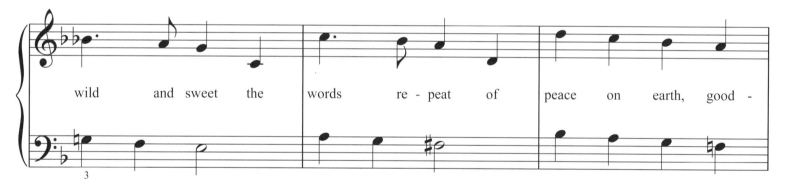

bel - fries of all Chris - ten - dom had rung so long the un -

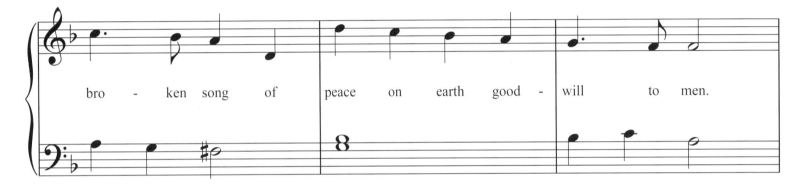

bro - ken song of peace on earth good - will to men.

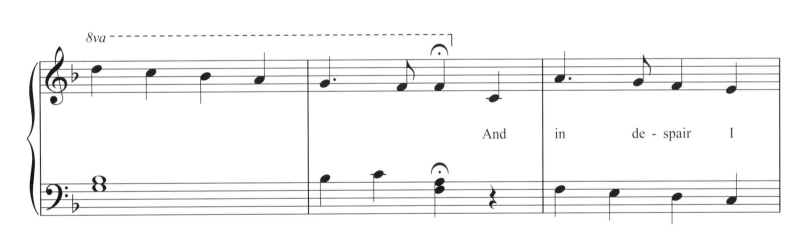

And in de - spair I

bowed my head. "There is no peace on earth," I said. "For

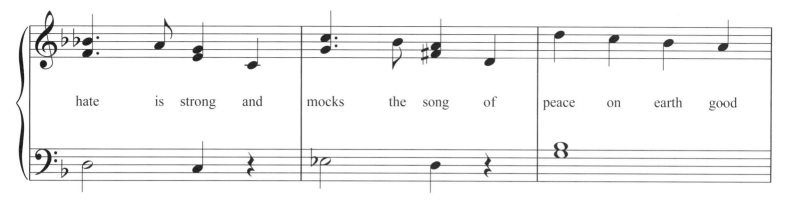

I WONDER AS I WANDER

By JOHN JACOB NILES

un - der the sky. When Mar - y birthed Je - sus, 'twas in a cow's stall, with

He was the King. I won - der as I wan - der, out un - der the sky, how

wise men and farm - ers and shep - herds and all. But high from God's heav - en a

Je - sus the Sav - ior did come for to die for poor on - 'ry peo - ple like

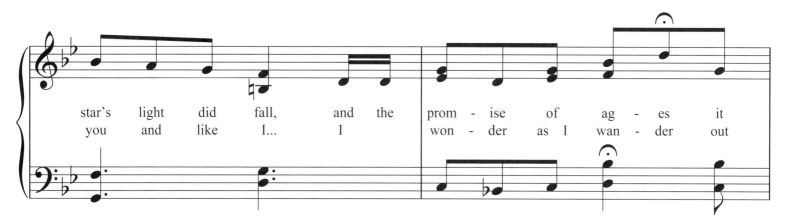

star's light did fall, and the prom - ise of ag - es it

you and like I... I won - der as I wan - der out

1.

then did re - call. If

2.

un - der the sky.

I'LL BE HOME FOR CHRISTMAS

Words and Music by KIM GANNON
and WALTER KENT

Moderately, in 2

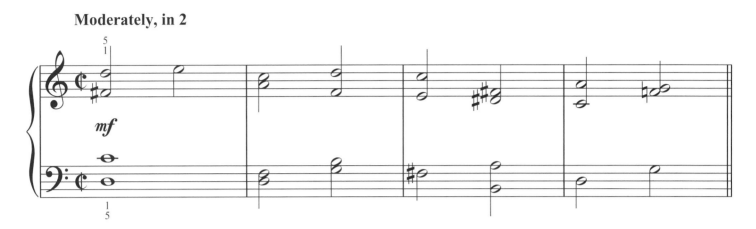

I'll be home for Christ - mas. _____ You can

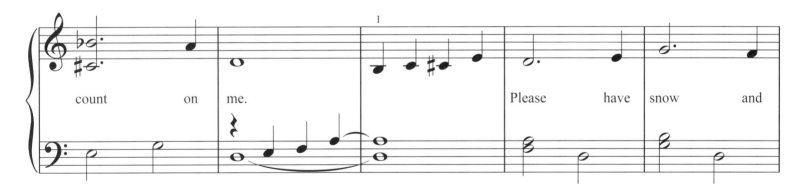

count on me. Please have snow and

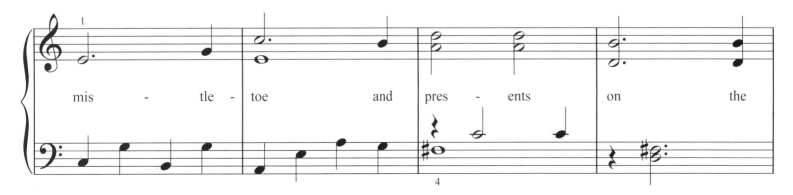

mis - tle - toe and pres - ents on the

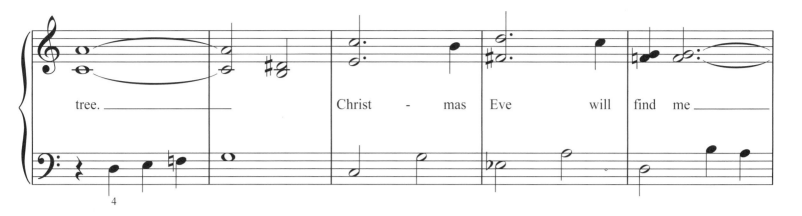

tree. _____ _____ Christ - mas Eve will find me _____

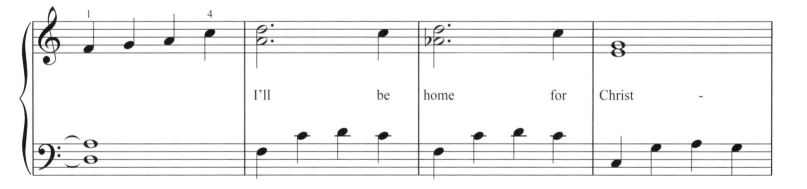

_____ where the love - light gleams.

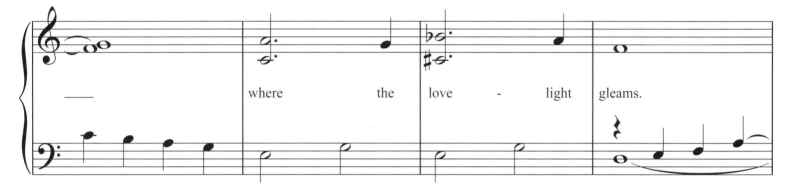

I'll be home for Christ -

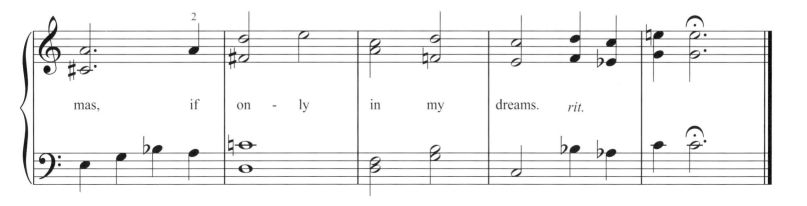

mas, if on - ly in my dreams. *rit.*

IT'S BEGINNING TO LOOK LIKE CHRISTMAS

By MEREDITH WILLSON

Moderately

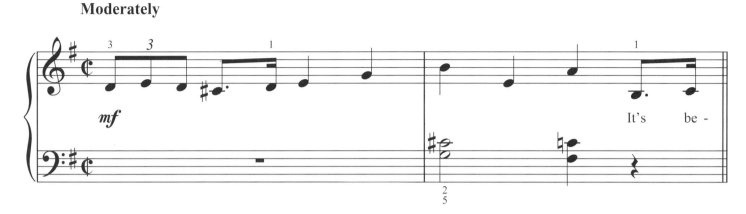

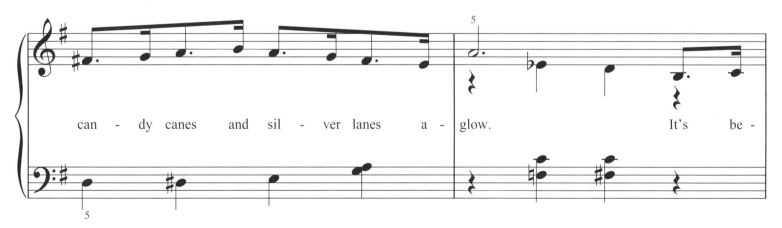

gin-ning to look a lot like Christ - mas, toys in ev - 'ry

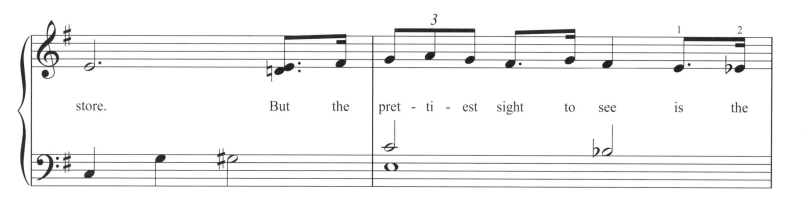

store. But the pret - ti - est sight to see is the

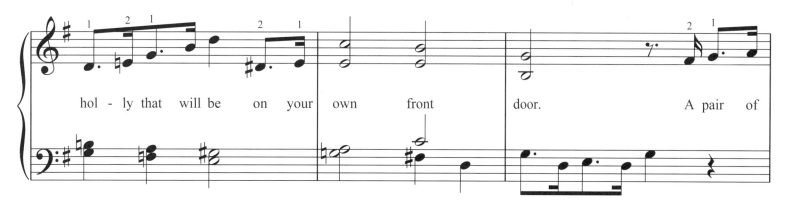

hol - ly that will be on your own front door. A pair of

hop - a - long boots and a pis - tol that shoots is the wish of Bar - ney and Ben.

82

Dolls that will talk and will go for a walk is the hope of Jan - ice and Jen. And

Mom and Dad can hard - ly wait for school to start a - gain. It's be -

gin - ning to look a lot like Christ - mas,

ev - 'ry - where you go. There's a tree in the Grand Ho - tel,

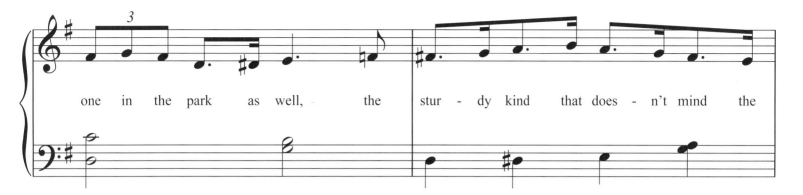

one in the park as well, the stur - dy kind that does - n't mind the

snow. It's be - gin-ning to look a lot like Christ - mas,

soon the bells will start. And the thing that will make them ring is the

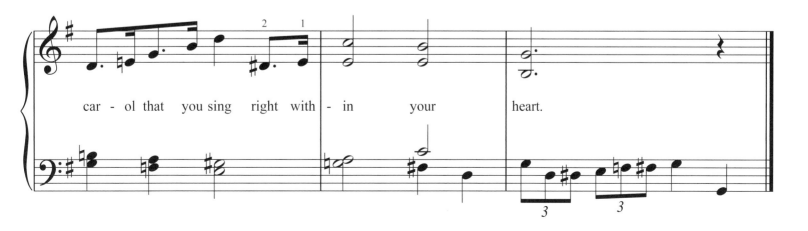

car - ol that you sing right with - in your heart.

LAST CHRISTMAS

Words and Music by
GEORGE MICHAEL

Moderately, with a steady beat

Last Christ-mas I gave you my heart, __ but the ver-y next day you

gave it a-way. __ This year, __ to save me from tears, __ I'll

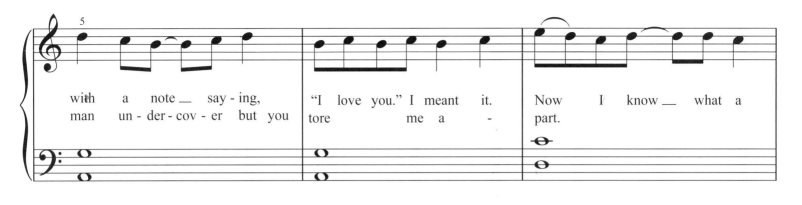

with a note _ say - ing,
man un - der - cov - er but you

"I love you." I meant it.
tore me a -

Now I know _ what a
part.

fool _ I've been. _ But if you
Oo, _____ now I've

kissed me now, _ I know you'd
found a real love. You'll nev - er

fool me a - gain. _

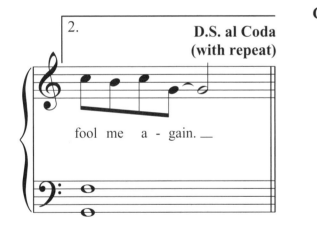

2.

D.S. al Coda
(with repeat)

fool me a - gain. _

CODA

spe - cial. A

face on a lov - er with a

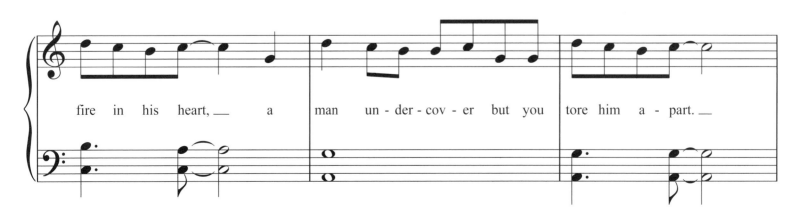

fire in his heart, _ a

man un - der - cov - er but you

tore him a - part. _

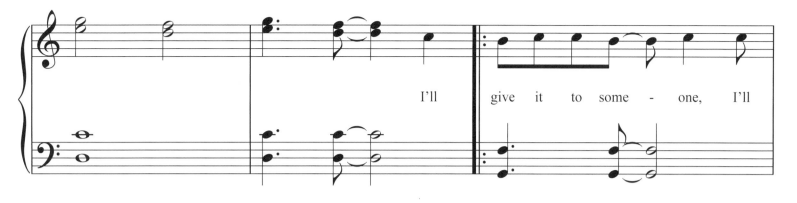

I'll give it to some - one, I'll

give it to some - one spe - cial, spe - cial.____

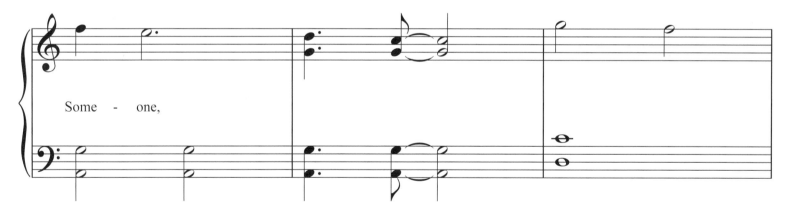

Some - one,

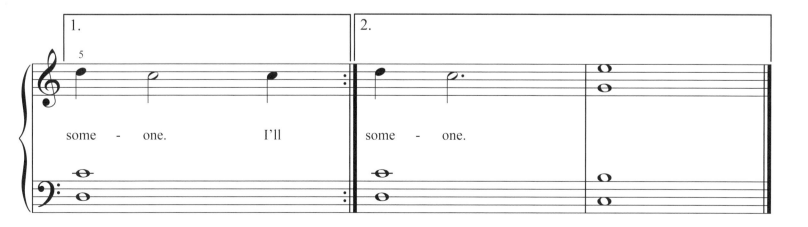

1.

some - one. I'll

2.

some - one.

LET IT SNOW! LET IT SNOW! LET IT SNOW!

Words by SAMMY CAHN
Music by JULE STYNE

Moderately, in 2

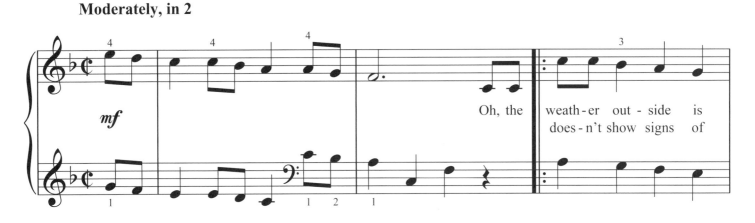

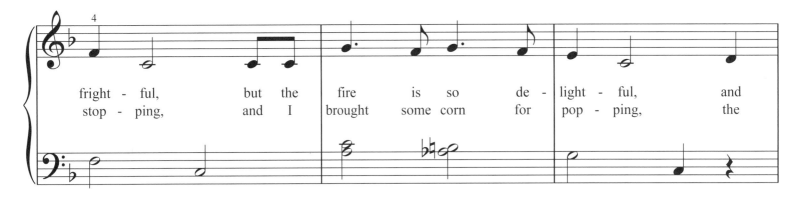

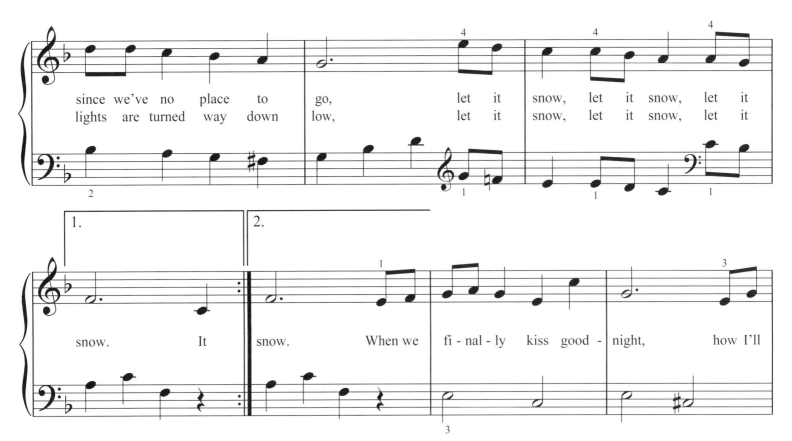

hate go - ing out in the storm; but if you'll real - ly hold me tight,

all the way home I'll be warm. The fire is slow - ly dy - ing, and my

dear, we're still good - bye - ing, but as long as you love me

so, let it snow, let it snow, let it snow.

THE LITTLE DRUMMER BOY

Words and Music by HARRY SIMEONE,
HENRY ONORATI and KATHERINE DAVIS

Moderately, in 2

to lay be - fore the King, pa -
that's fit to give our King, pa -

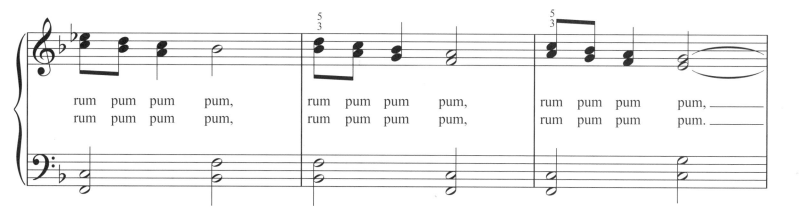

rum pum pum pum,   rum pum pum pum,   rum pum pum pum, ___
rum pum pum pum,   rum pum pum pum,   rum pum pum pum. ___

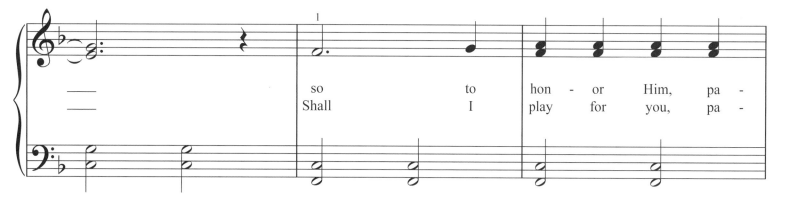

so   to hon - or Him, pa -
Shall   I play for you, pa -

1.

rum pum pum pum, ___
rum pum pum pum, ___

when we come. ___
on ___ my drum? ___

2.

Mar - y

nod - ded, pa - rum pum pum pum.

The ox and lamb kept time, pa - rum pum pum pum.

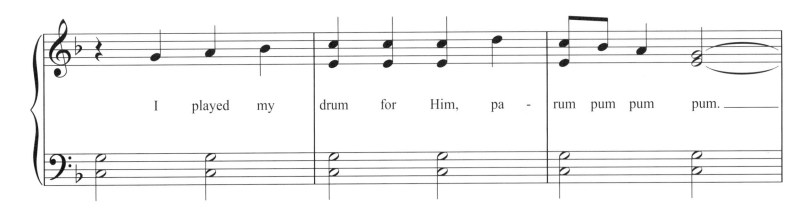

I played my drum for Him, pa - rum pum pum pum.

I played my best for Him, pa - rum pum pum pum,

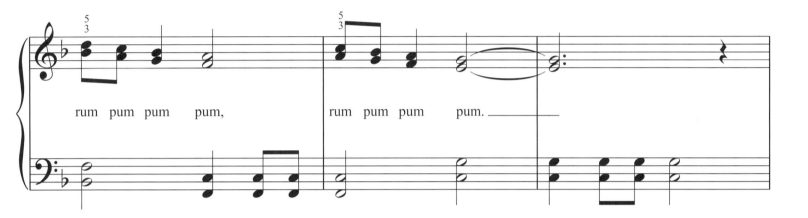

rum pum pum pum, rum pum pum pum.

Then He smiled at me, pa - rum pum pum pum,

me and my drum.

rit.

A MARSHMALLOW WORLD

Words by CARL SIGMAN
Music by PETER DE ROSE

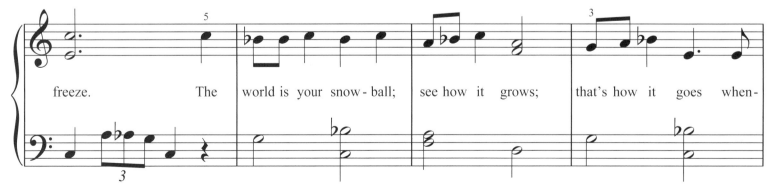

ev - er it snows. The world is your snow - ball; just for a song, get out and roll it a -

long. It's a yum, yum - my world made for sweet - hearts; _____ take a

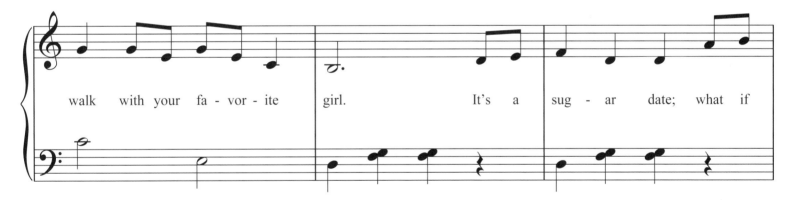

walk with your fa - vor - ite girl. It's a sug - ar date; what if

spring is late? In win - ter, it's a marsh - mal - low world.

MARY, DID YOU KNOW?

Words and Music by MARK LOWRY
and BUDDY GREENE

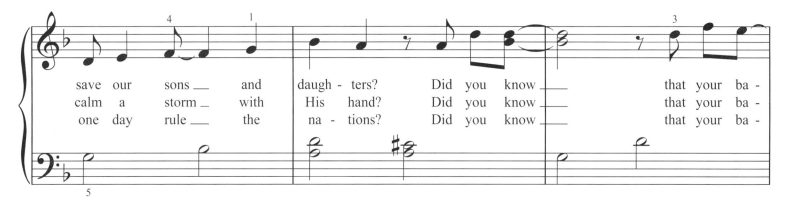

- by boy ___ has come to make ___ you new? This child ___
- by boy ___ has walked where an - gels trod, and when you
- by boy ___ was heav - en's per - fect Lamb, and the sleep -

To Coda ⊕

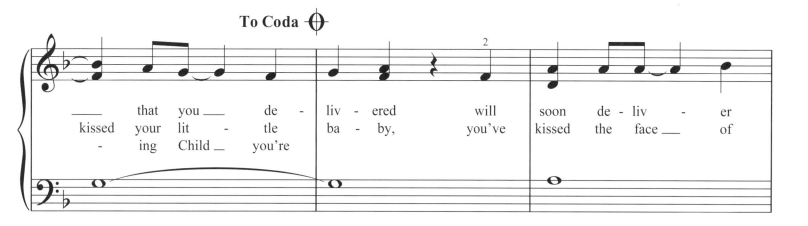

___ that you ___ de - liv - ered will soon de - liv - er
kissed your lit - tle ba - by, you've kissed the face ___ of
- ing Child ___ you're

1.   2.

you.   Mar - y, did you   God? Oh, Mar - y did you know?

The blind will see, ___ the

deaf will hear, __ the dead will live __ a - gain, the lame will leap, __ the

D.S. al Coda

dumb will speak __ the prais - es of ___ the Lamb. Mar - y, did you

CODA

hold - ing is the great I AM?

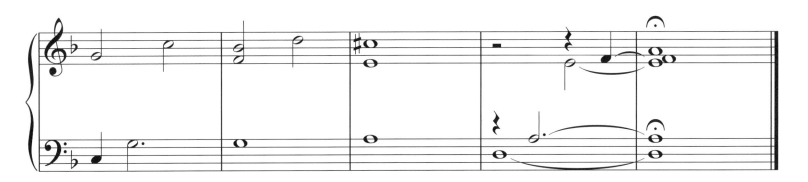

MERRY CHRISTMAS, BABY

Words and Music by LOU BAXTER
and JOHNNY MOORE

Slow Blues

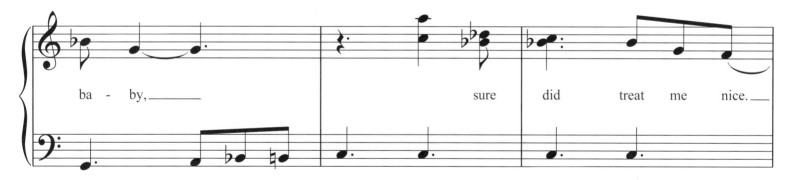

Christ - mas, ba - by, sure___ did___ treat me nice.___

___ Gave me a dia -

mond ring for Christ - mas, now I'm liv - ing in par - a - dise.___

___ Well, I'm

feel - ing might - y fine;_____ got good mu - sic on my ra - di - o.__

_____ Well, I'm feel -

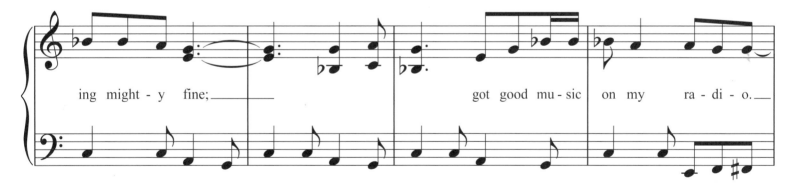

ing might - y fine;_____ got good mu - sic on my ra - di - o.__

_____ Well, I

wan - na kiss you, ba - by,

while you're stand - ing 'neath the mis - tle - toe.

I said mer -

- ry Christ - mas, ba - by,

yes, you sure did treat me nice._

Mer - ry,

mer - ry Christ - mas, ba - by,

well, you sure___ did___ treat me

nice.

Gave me a dia - mond

ring for Christ - mas,

now I'm liv - ing in_____ par - a - dise.___

THE MOST WONDERFUL TIME OF THE YEAR

Words and Music by EDDIE POLA
and GEORGE WYLE

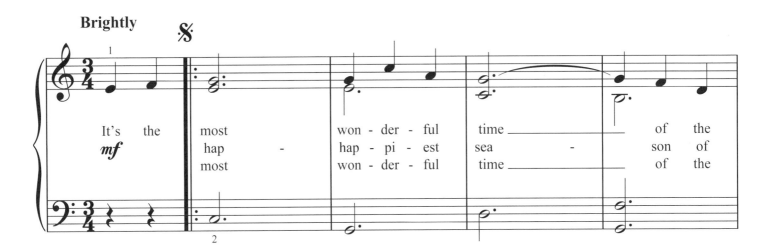

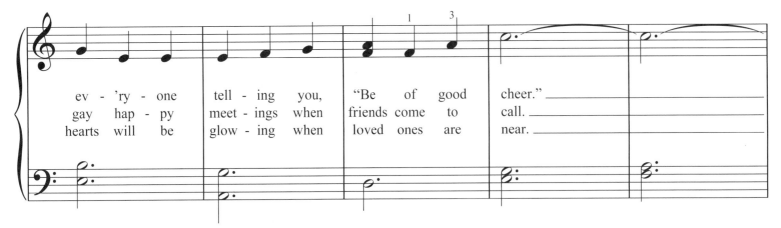

car - ol - ing   out   in   the   snow. _____   There'll   be   scar - y   ghost

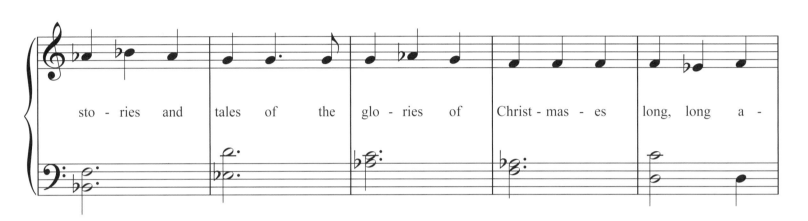

sto - ries   and   tales   of   the   glo - ries   of   Christ - mas - es   long,   long   a -

D.S. al Coda

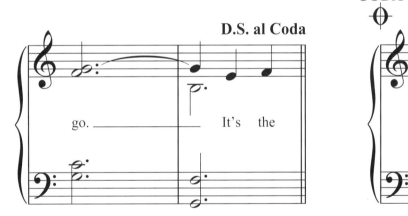

go. _____   It's   the

CODA

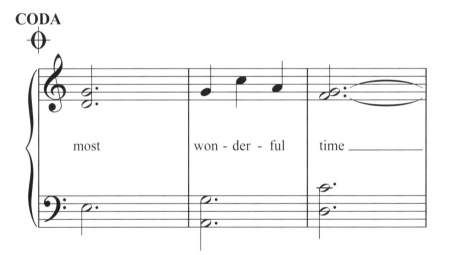

most   won - der - ful   time _____

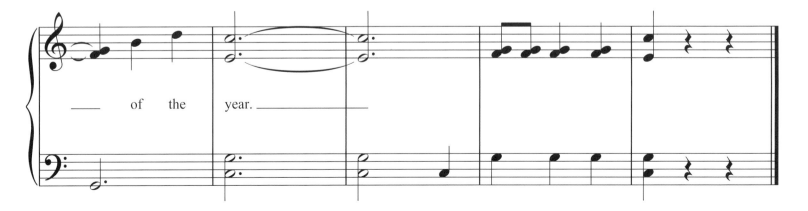

_____   of   the   year. _____

RIVER

Words and Music by
JONI MITCHELL

Slowly

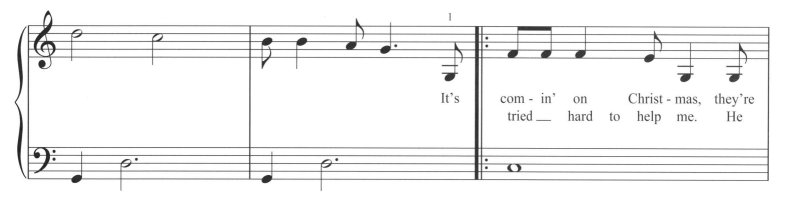

It's   com - in'   on   Christ - mas,   they're
tried __ hard   to   help   me.   He

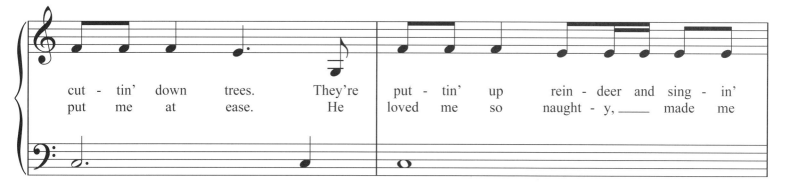

cut - tin'   down   trees.   They're   put - tin'   up   rein - deer   and   sing - in'
put   me   at   ease.   He   loved   me   so   naught - y, __ made   me

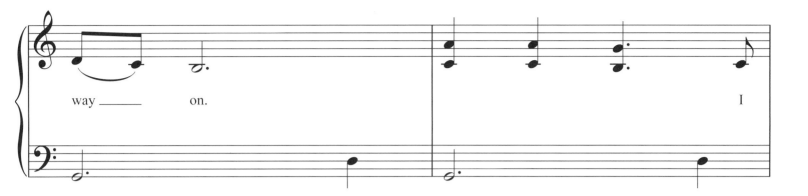

way _____ on.   I

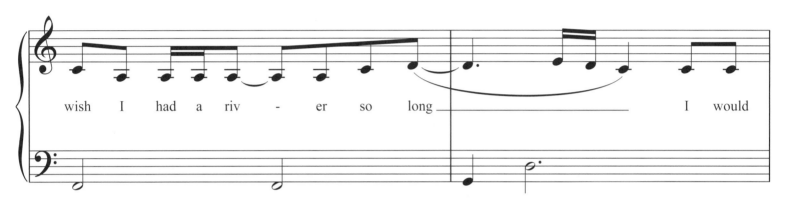

wish I had a riv - er so long _____ I would

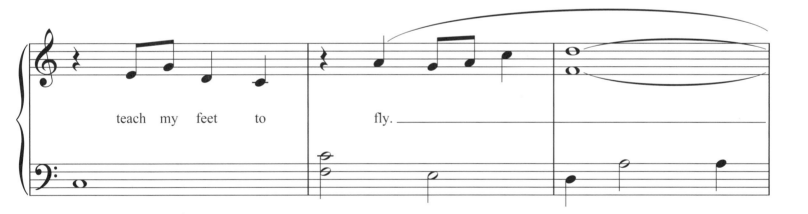

teach my feet to   fly. _____

_____   Oh, I   wish I had a riv - er   I could skate a-

way   on.

I   made _ my __ ba - by _
I   made _ my __ ba - by say _

__   cry. _____
__   good - bye.

1.   2.

He   It's

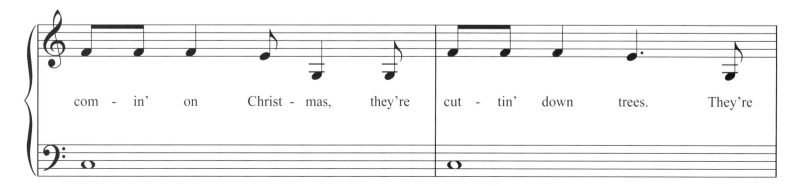

com - in' on Christ - mas, they're cut - tin' down trees. They're

put - tin' up   rein - deer and sing - in'   songs   of   joy   and   peace.

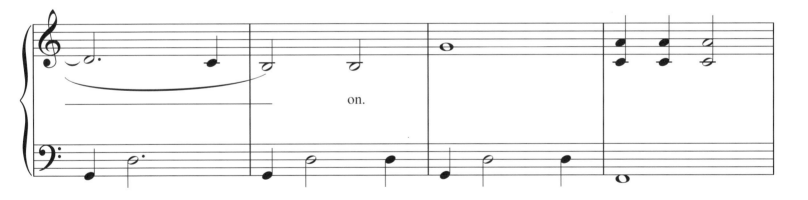

Oh, I wish I ___ had a riv - er   I could skate   a - way ___

on.

rit.

NUTTIN' FOR CHRISTMAS

Words and Music by ROY C. BENNETT
and SID TEPPER

Moderately fast

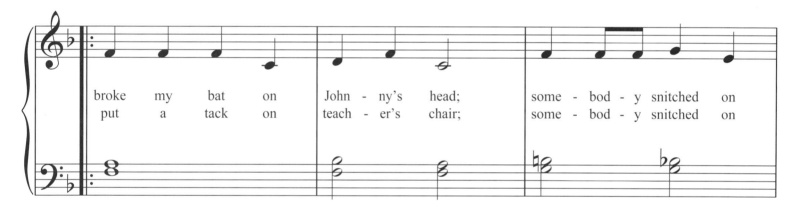

broke my bat on Joh - ny's head; some - bod - y snitched on
put a tack on teach - er's chair; some - bod - y snitched on

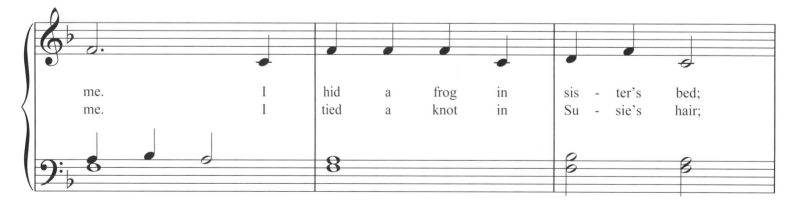

me. I hid a frog in sis - ter's bed;
me. I tied a knot in Su - sie's hair;

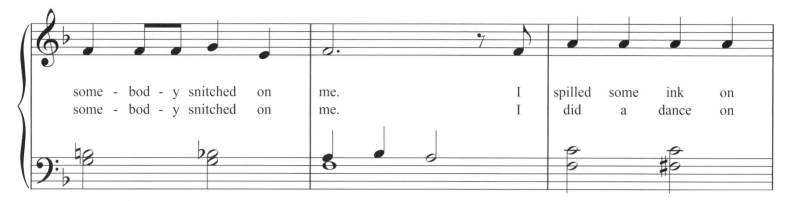

some - bod - y snitched on me.   I spilled some ink on
some - bod - y snitched on me.   I did a dance on

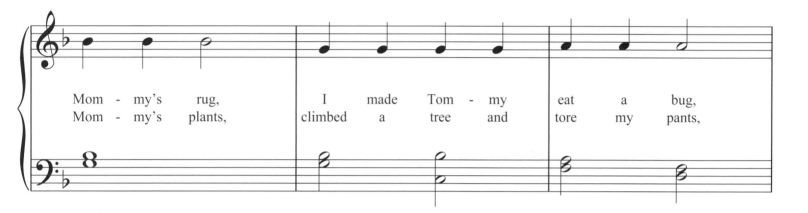

Mom - my's rug,   I made Tom - my eat a bug,
Mom - my's plants, climbed a tree and tore my pants,

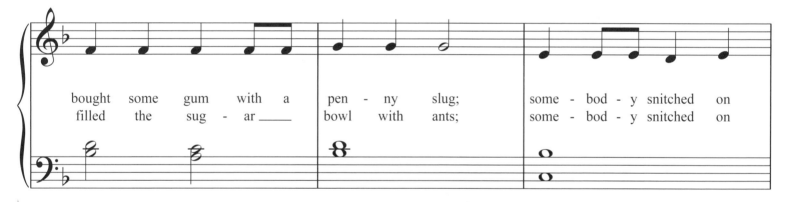

bought some gum with a pen - ny slug; some - bod - y snitched on
filled the sug - ar bowl with ants; some - bod - y snitched on

me.   Oh, I'm get - tin' nut - tin' for
me.   So,

Christ - mas. _____ Mom - my and

Dad - dy are mad. _____ I'm

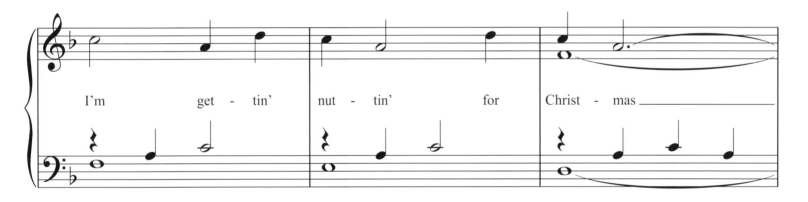

I'm get - tin' nut - tin' for Christ - mas _____

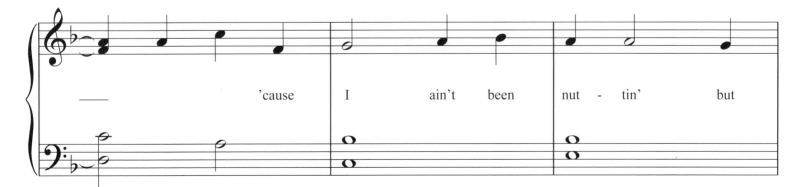

_____ 'cause I ain't been nut - tin' but

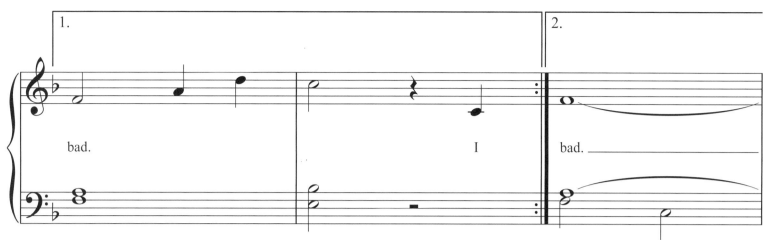

bad.   I   bad.

—   So you bet - ter be good, what - ev - er you do, 'cause

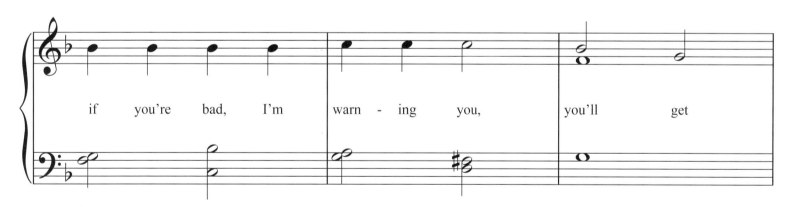

if you're bad, I'm warn - ing you, you'll get

nut - tin'   for   Christ - mas.

PLEASE COME HOME FOR CHRISTMAS

Words and Music by CHARLES BROWN
and GENE REDD

Slow and bluesy

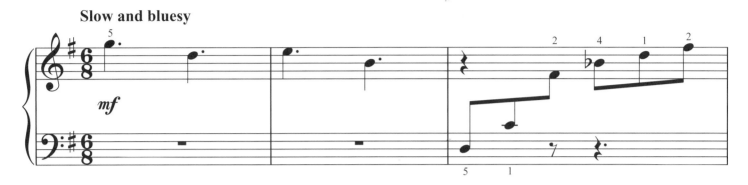

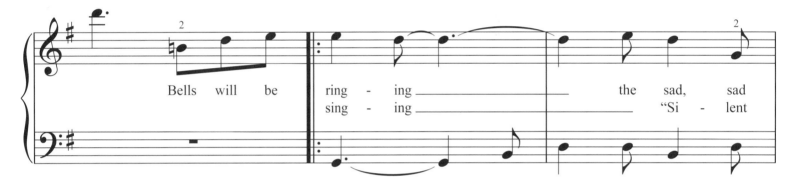

Bells will be ring - ing _____ the sad, sad
sing - ing _____ "Si - lent

news, _____ oh _____ what a Christ - mas _____
Night," _____ Christ - mas car - ols _____

_____ to have the blues! _____ My ba - by's
_____ by can - dle - light. Please come home for

gone, _____
Christ - mas, ___

I have no friends _____
please come home for Christ - mas; _____

1.

_____ to wish me greet - ings _____ once ___ a -
_____ if not for

gain. _____

Choirs will be

2.

Christ - mas, ___

by New Year's night. _____

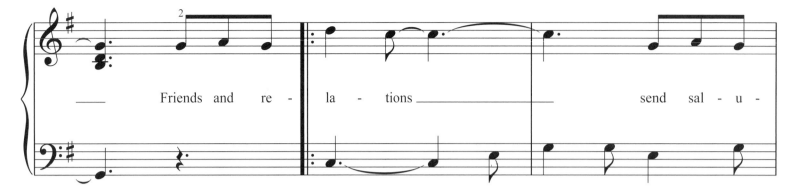

Friends and re - la - tions _____ send sal - u -

ta - tions _____ sure _____ as the

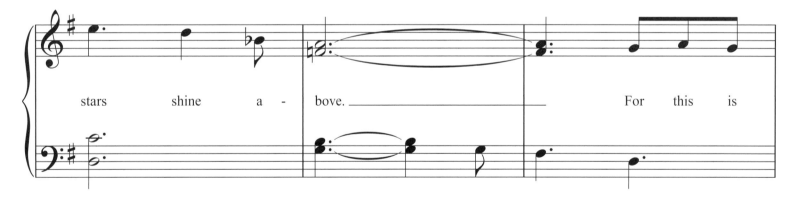

stars shine a - bove. _____ For this is

Christ - mas, _____ yes, Christ - mas, my dear. _____

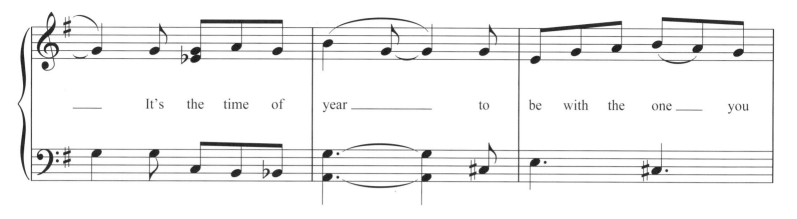

It's the time of year _____ to be with the one ___ you

love. So won't you tell me _____

___ you'll nev - er - more roam, _____ Christ - mas and

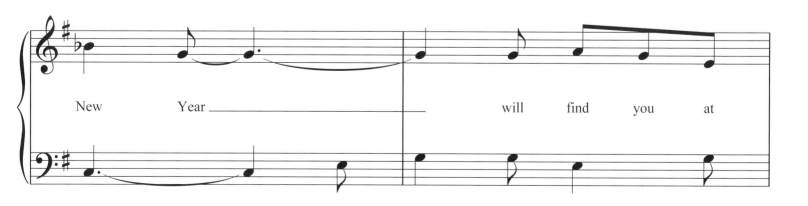

New Year _____ will find you at

home. _____ There'll be no more sor - row ____

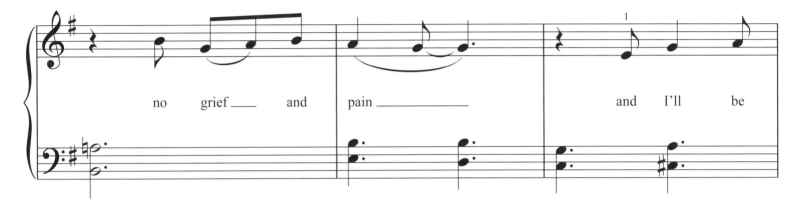

no grief ____ and pain _____ and I'll be

hap - py, hap - py once _____ a - gain.

1.

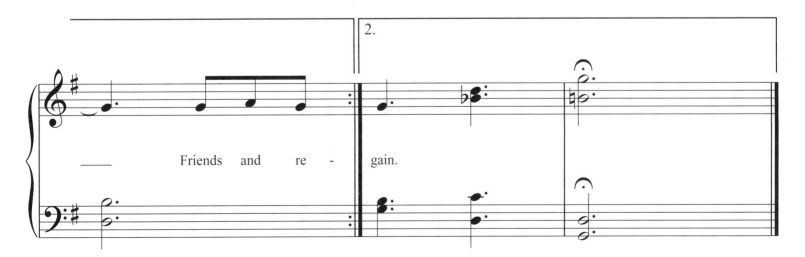

____ Friends and re - gain.

2.

SANTA BABY

By JOAN JAVITS,
PHIL SPRINGER and TONY SPRINGER

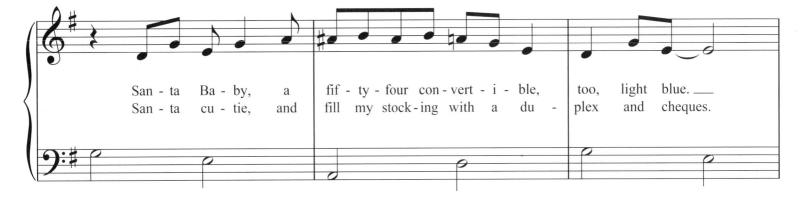

Santa Ba - by, a fif - ty - four con - vert - i - ble, too, light blue. ___
San - ta cu - tie, and fill my stock - ing with a du - plex and cheques.

I'll wait up for you, dear San - ta Ba - by, so hur - ry down the chim - ney to -
Sign your X on the line, San - ta cut - ie, and hur - ry down the chim - ney to -

night.
night.
Think of all the fun I've missed. ___
Come and trim my Christ - mas tree ___

Think of all the fel - las that I have - n't kissed. ___ Next year I could be
with some dec - o - ra - tions bought at Tif - fa - ny. ___ I real - ly do be -

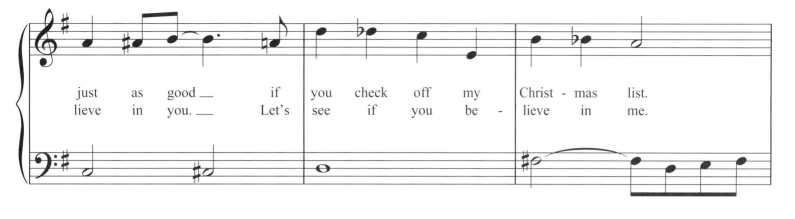

just as good ___ if you check off my Christ - mas list.
lieve in you. ___ Let's see if you be - lieve in me.

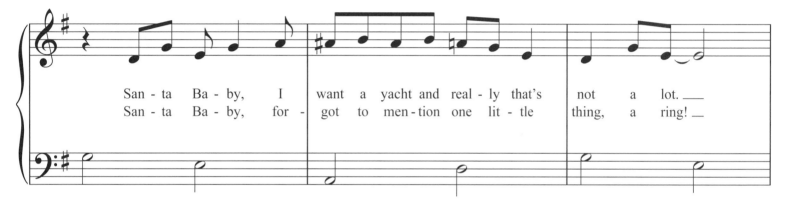

San - ta Ba - by, I want a yacht and real - ly that's not a lot. ___
San - ta Ba - by, for - got to men - tion one lit - tle thing, a ring! ___

Been an an - gel all year, San - ta Ba - by, so hur - ry down the chim - ney to -
I don't mean on the phone, San - ta Ba - by, so hur - ry down the chim - ney to -

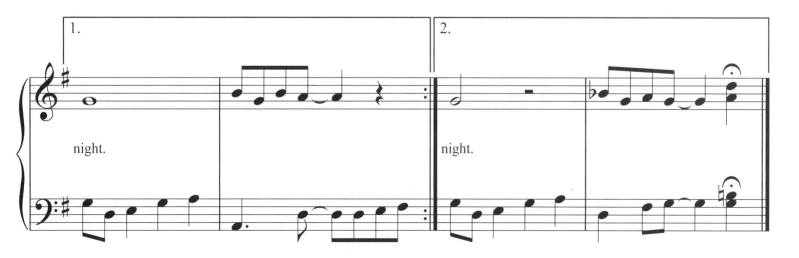

1.
night.

2.
night.

RUDOLPH THE RED-NOSED REINDEER

Music and Lyrics by
JOHNNY MARKS

Freely

You know Dash-er and Danc-er and Pranc-er and Vix-en,

Com-et and Cu-pid and Don-ner and Blitz-en, but do you re-

call the most fa-mous rein-deer of all?

Moderate Swing

Ru-dolph the red-nosed rein-deer had a ver-y shin-y
All of the oth-er rein-deer used to laugh and call him

1.

nose,
names.

and if you ev - er saw it,
They nev - er let poor Ru - dolph

you would e - ven say it

2.

glows.

join in an - y rein - deer games.

Then one fog - gy Christ - mas Eve, San - ta came to say,

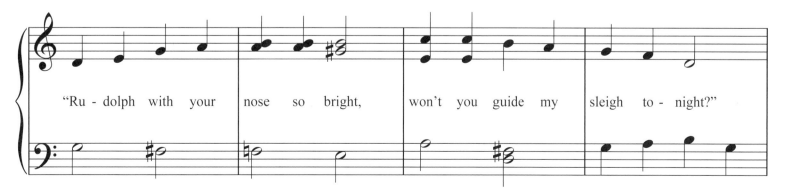

"Ru - dolph with your nose so bright, won't you guide my sleigh to - night?"

Then how the rein - deer loved him, as they shout - ed out with

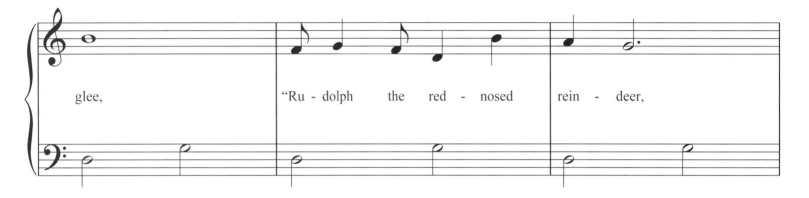

glee, "Ru - dolph the red - nosed rein - deer,

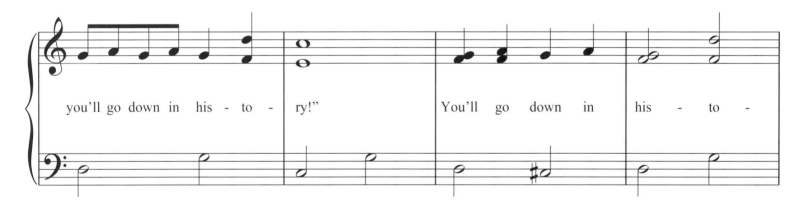

you'll go down in his - to - ry!" You'll go down in his - to -

ry! _____

RUN RUDOLPH RUN

Music and Lyrics by JOHNNY MARKS
and MARVIN BRODIE

Fast Rock 'n' Roll

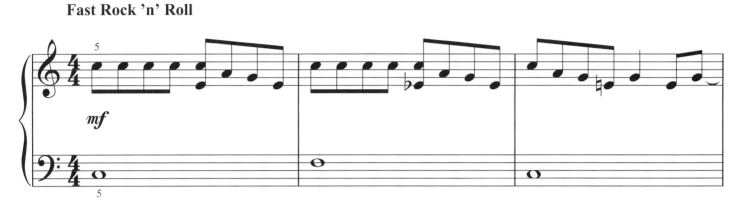

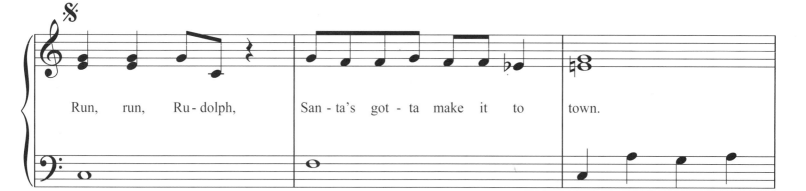

Run, run, Ru - dolph, Santa's got - ta make it to town.

San - ta, make him hur - ry, tell him he can take the free - way down.

Run, run, Ru - dolph, 'cause I'm

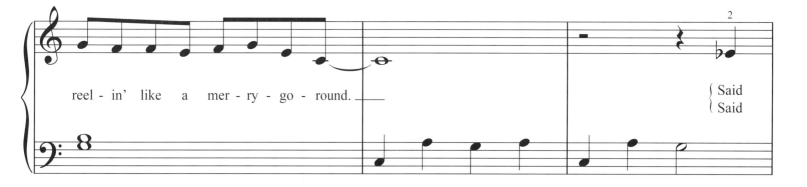

reel - in' like a mer - ry - go - round. Said / Said

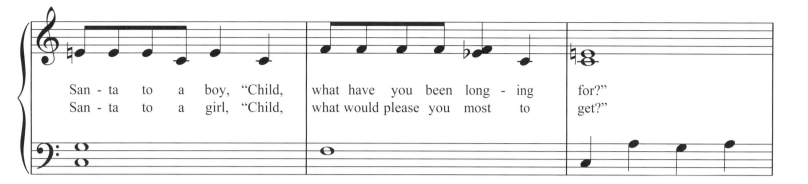

Santa to a boy, "Child, what have you been long - ing for?"
San - ta to a girl, "Child, what would please you most to get?"

"All I want for Christ-mas is a rock 'n' roll e - lec - tric gui - tar." __
"A lit - tle ba - by doll __ that can cry, __ sleep, __ drink __ and wet." __

And then a - way went Ru - dolph,
And then a - way went Ru - dolph,

whiz - zin' like a shoot - ing star. __
whiz - zin' like a Sa - ber jet. __

Run, run Ru-dolph, Santa's got-ta make it to town.

Santa, make him hur-ry, tell him he can take the free-way down.

Run, run, Ru-dolph,

To Coda

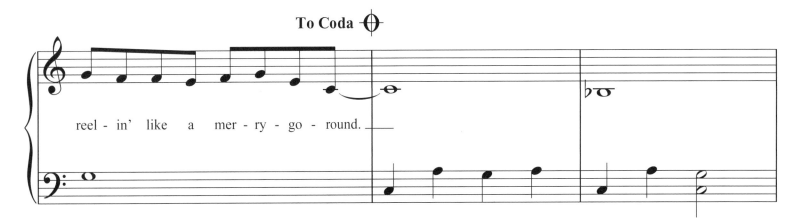

reel-in' like a mer-ry-go-round.

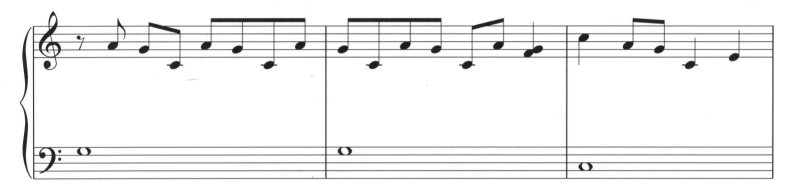

D.S. al Coda

CODA

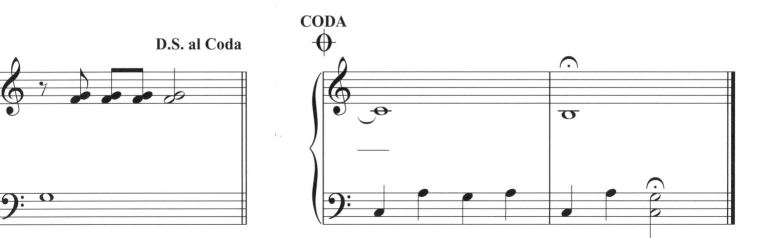

SANTA CLAUS IS COMIN' TO TOWN

Words by HAVEN GILLESPIE
Music by J. FRED COOTS

You bet-ter watch out, you

bet-ter not cry, bet-ter not pout, I'm tell-ing you why:

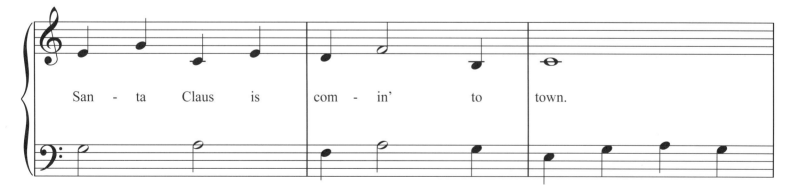

San-ta Claus is com-in' to town.

He's mak - ing a list and check - ing it twice,

gon - na find out who's naugh - ty and nice, San - ta Claus is

com - in' to town. He

sees you when you're sleep - in', he knows when you're a -

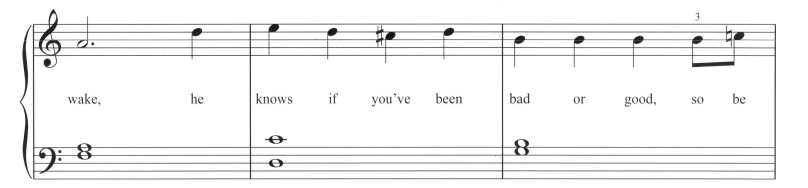

wake,   he   knows   if   you've   been   bad   or   good,   so   be

good   for   good - ness'   sake.   You   bet - ter   watch   out,   you

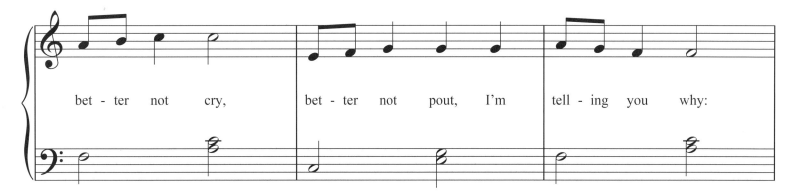

bet - ter   not   cry,   bet - ter   not   pout,   I'm   tell - ing   you   why:

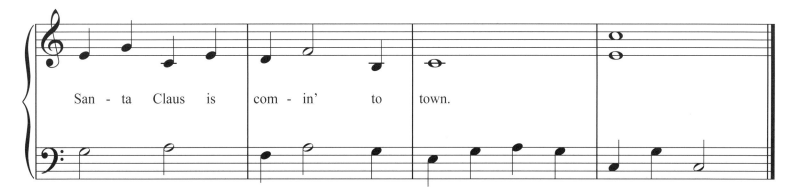

San - ta   Claus   is   com - in'   to   town.

SILVER BELLS

from the Paramount Picture THE LEMON DROP KID

Words and Music by JAY LIVINGSTON
and RAY EVANS

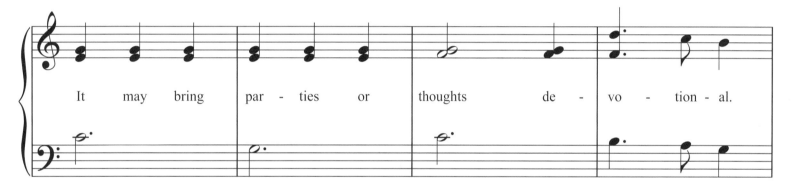

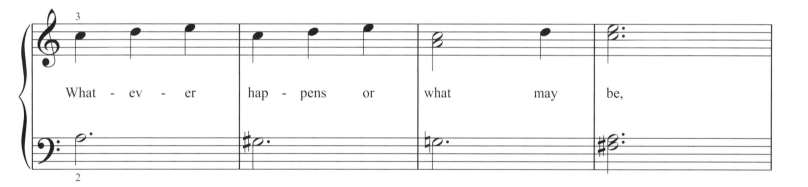

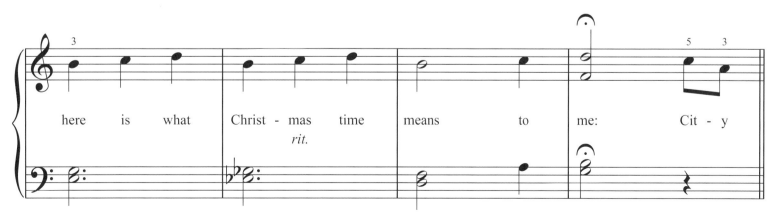

Moderately

side - walks, bus - y side - walks dressed in hol - i - day style. In the
street lights, e - ven stop - lights blink a bright red and green as the

air there's a feel - ing of Christ - mas. Chil - dren
shop - pers rush home with their treas - ures. Hear the

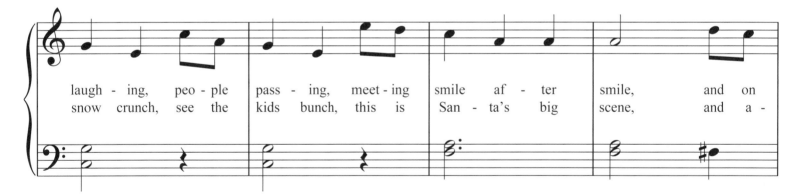

laugh - ing, peo - ple pass - ing, meet - ing smile af - ter smile, and on
snow crunch, see the kids bunch, this is San - ta's big scene, and a -

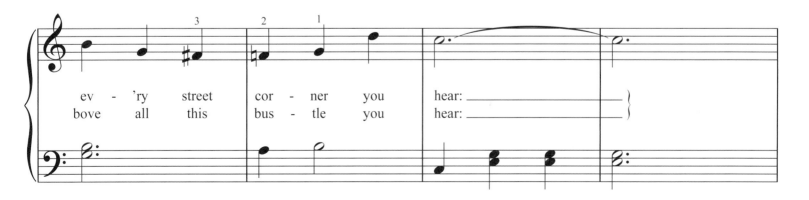

ev - 'ry street cor - ner you hear:
bove all this bus - tle you hear:

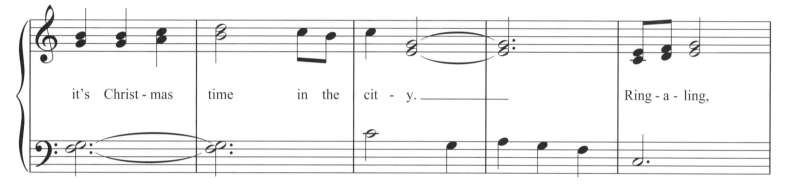

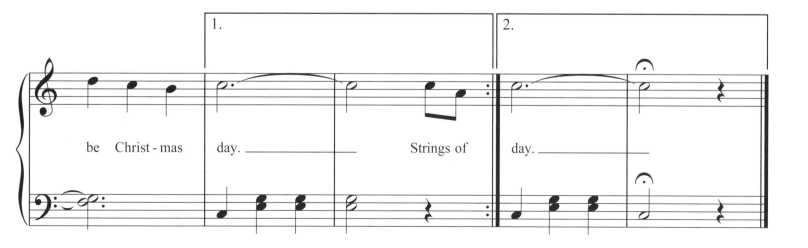

SILVER AND GOLD

Music and Lyrics by
JOHNNY MARKS

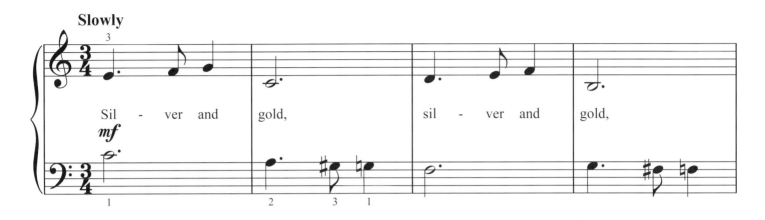

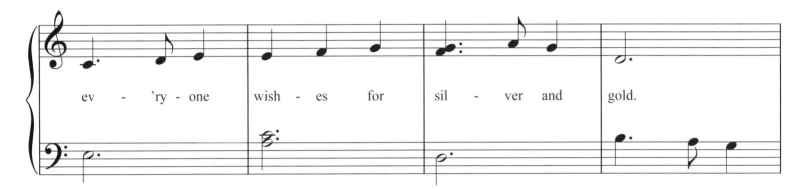

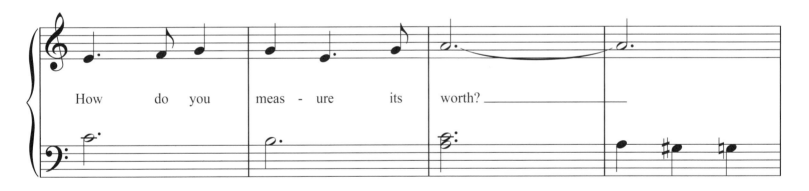

Sil - ver and gold, sil - ver and gold,

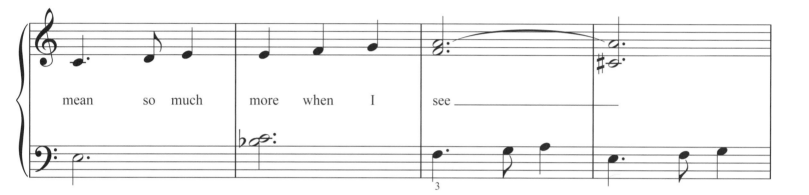

mean so much more when I see _____

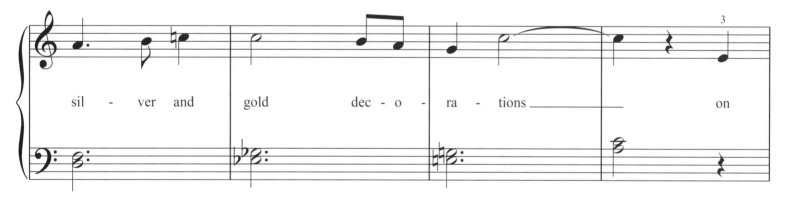

sil - ver and gold dec - o - ra - tions _____ on

ev - 'ry Christ - mas tree.

THIS CHRISTMAS

Words and Music by DONNY HATHAWAY
and NADINE McKINNOR

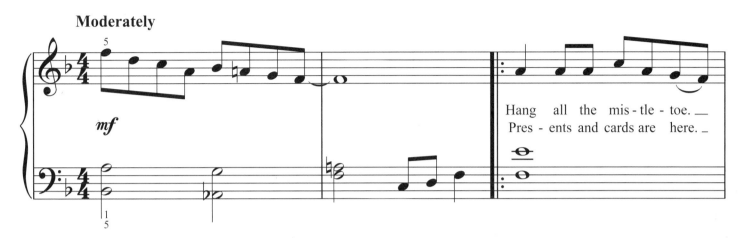

Hang all the mis-tle-toe. __
Pres - ents and cards are here. __

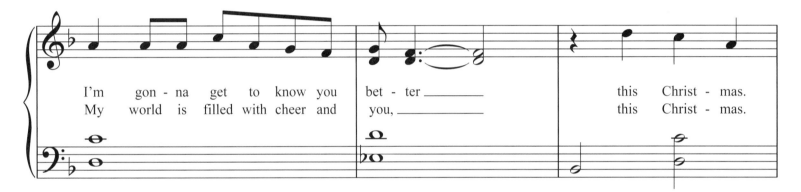

I'm gon - na get to know you bet - ter __ this Christ - mas.
My world is filled with cheer and you, __ this Christ - mas.

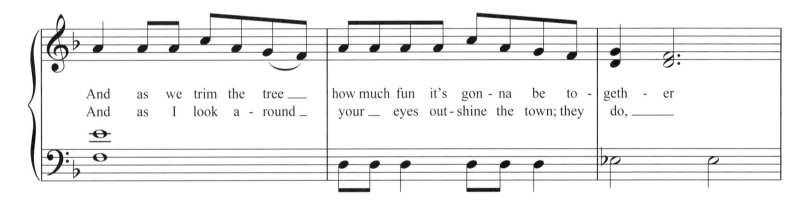

And as we trim the tree __ how much fun it's gon - na be to - geth - er
And as I look a - round __ your __ eyes out - shine the town; they do, __

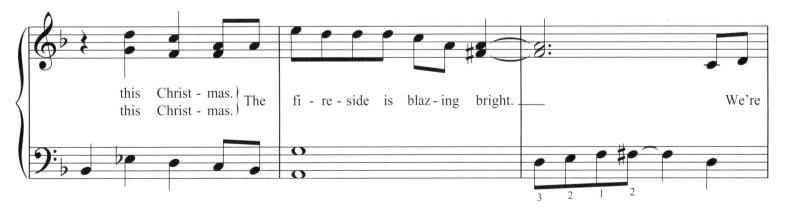

this Christ - mas.
this Christ - mas. } The fi - re - side is blaz - ing bright. __ We're

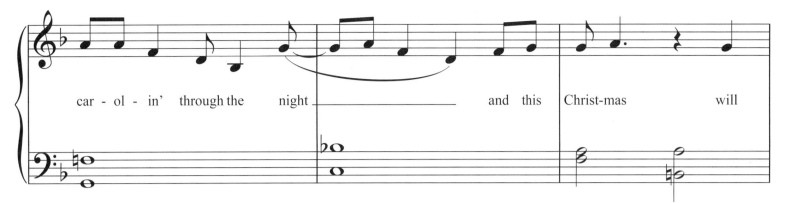

car - ol - in' through the night _____ and this Christ-mas will

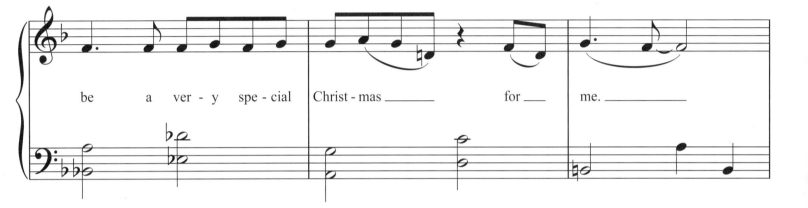

be a ver - y spe - cial Christ - mas _____ for ___ me. _____

1., 2.

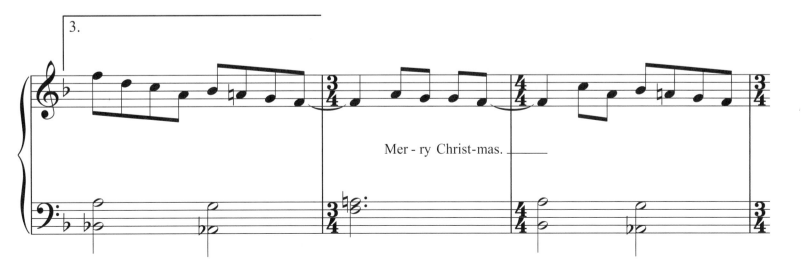

3.

Mer - ry Christ-mas. _____

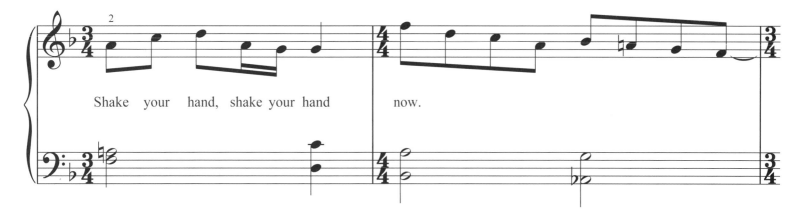

Shake your hand, shake your hand   now.

Wish your broth - er   mer - ry Christ - mas

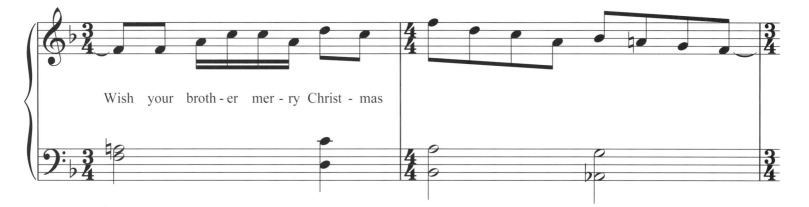

all   o - ver the land   now.

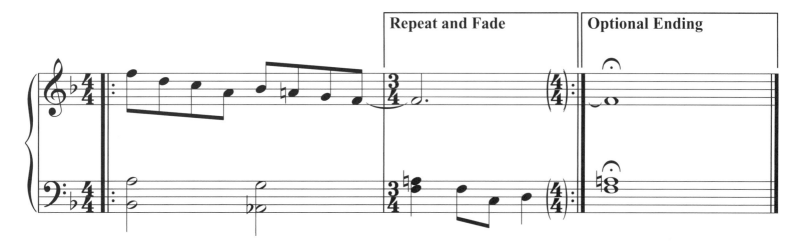

Repeat and Fade   **Optional Ending**

SLEIGH RIDE

Music by LEROY ANDERSON
Words by MITCHELL PARISH

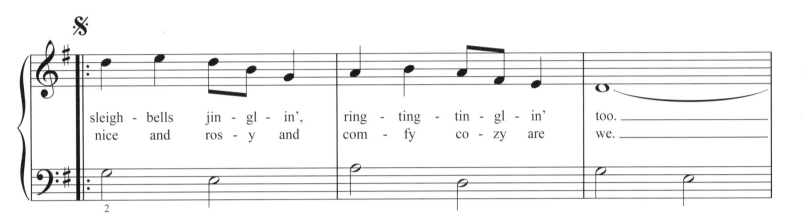

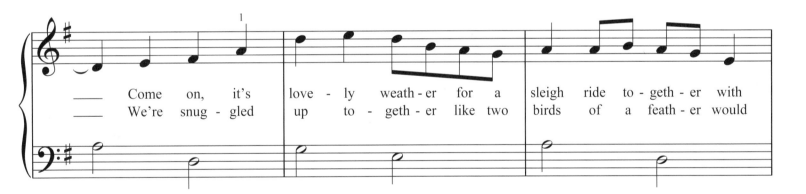

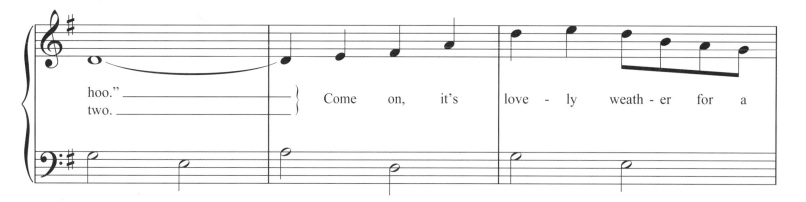

hoo."
two.

Come on, it's love - ly weath - er for a

To Coda ⊕

sleigh ride to - geth - er with you. Gid - dy -

yap, gid - dy - yap, gid - dy - yap, let's go. Let's look at the

show. We're rid - ing in a won - der - land of

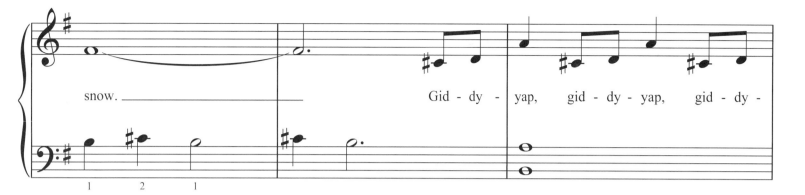

snow. _____

Gid - dy - yap, gid - dy - yap, gid - dy -

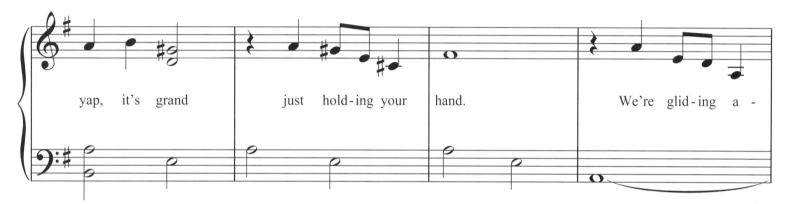

yap, it's grand   just hold-ing your   hand.   We're glid-ing a -

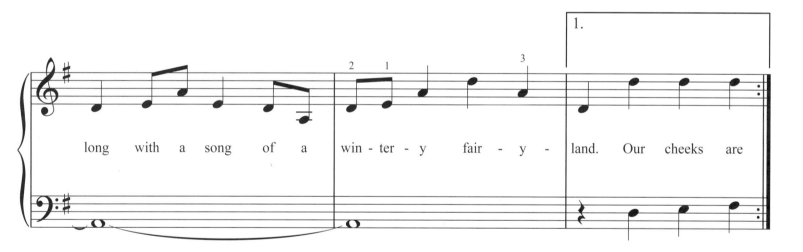

long with a song of a   win-ter - y   fair - y - land. Our cheeks are

D.S. al Coda

land. Our cheeks are

CODA

you. _____

SOMEWHERE IN MY MEMORY

from the Twentieth Century Fox Motion Picture HOME ALONE

Words by LESLIE BRICUSSE
Music by JOHN WILLIAMS

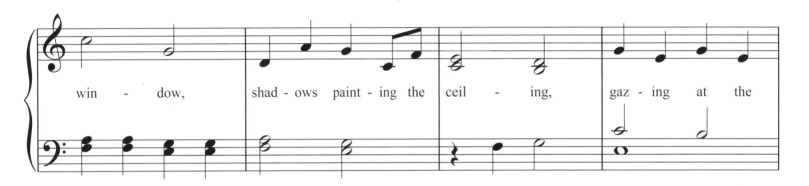

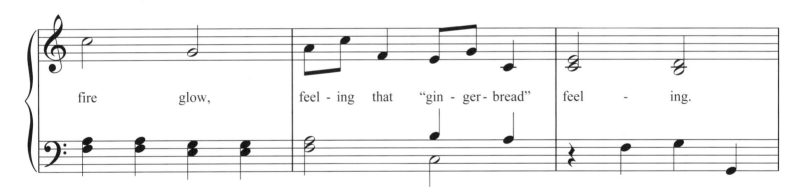

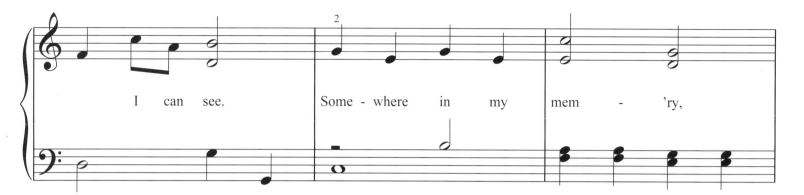

I can see. Some - where in my mem - 'ry,

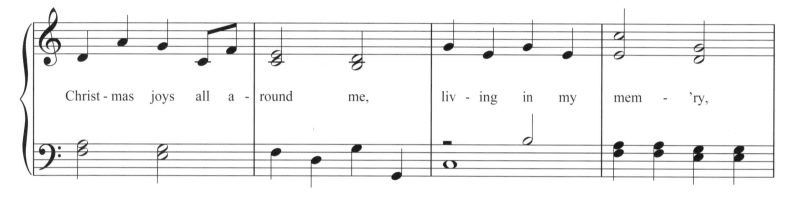

Christ - mas joys all a - round me, liv - ing in my mem - 'ry,

all of the mu - sic, all of the mag - ic, all of the fam - 'ly

home here with me.

WE NEED A LITTLE CHRISTMAS

from MAME

Music and Lyric by
JERRY HERMAN

Brightly

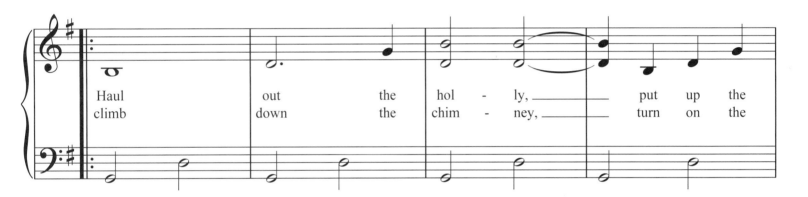

Haul out the hol - ly, _____ put up the
climb down the chim - ney, _____ turn on the

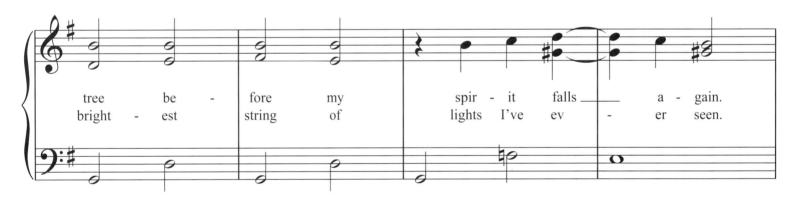

tree be - fore my spir - it falls _____ a - gain.
bright - est string of lights I've ev - er seen.

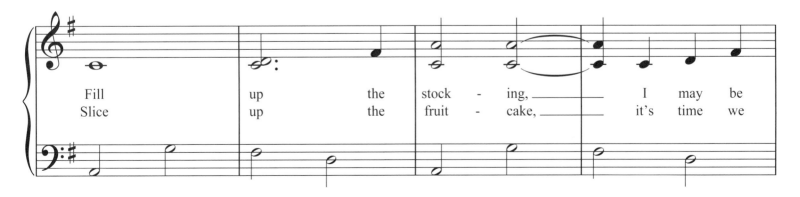

Fill up the stock - ing, _____ I may be
Slice up the fruit - cake, _____ it's time we

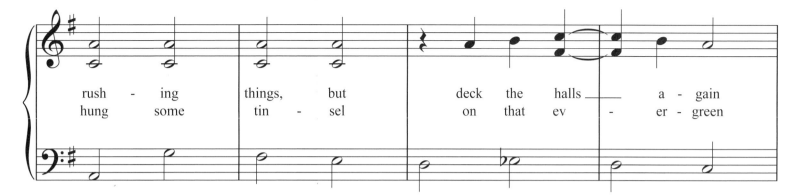

rush - ing things, but deck the halls ____ a - gain
hung some tin - sel on that ev _ - er - green

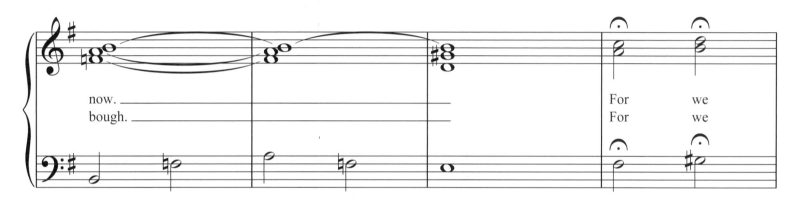

now. _____ For we
bough. _____ For we

need a lit - tle Christ - mas, right this ver - y
need a lit - tle mu - sic, need a lit - tle

min - ute, can - dles in the win - dow,
laugh - ter, need a lit - tle sing - ing

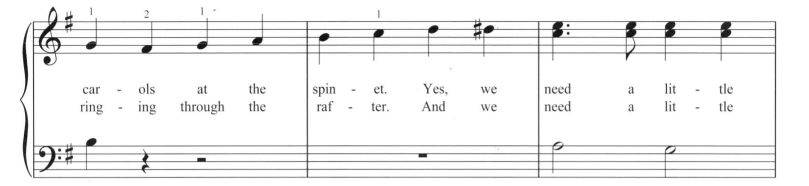

car - ols at the spin - et. Yes, we need a lit - tle
ring - ing through the raf - ter. And we need a lit - tle

1.

Christ - mas, right this ver - y min - ute. It has - n't snowed a
snap - py "Hap - py ev - er af - ter." We

sin - gle flur - ry, but San - ta, dear, we're in a hur - ry. So

2.

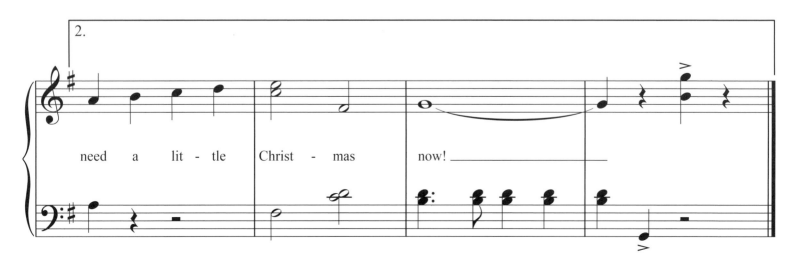

need a lit - tle Christ - mas now!

WHAT ARE YOU DOING NEW YEAR'S EVE?

By FRANK LOESSER

Moderately slow

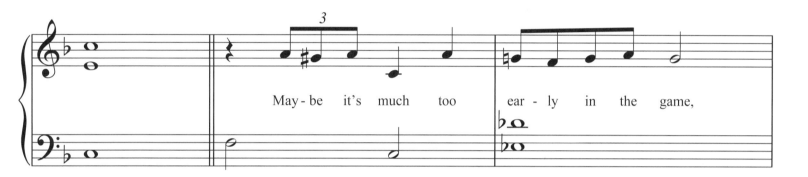

May - be it's much too ear - ly in the game,

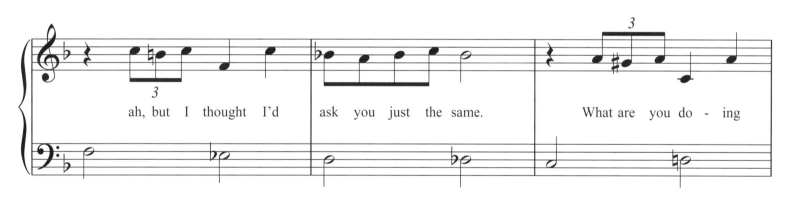

ah, but I thought I'd ask you just the same. What are you do - ing

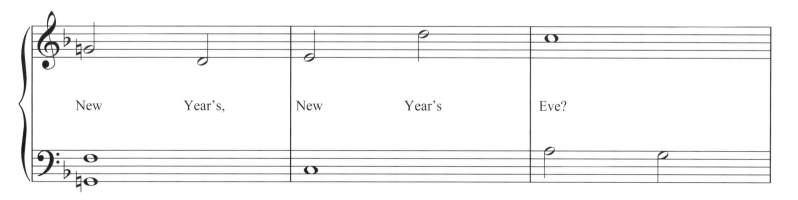

New Year's, New Year's Eve?

152

Won - der whose arms will hold you good and tight, when it's ex - act - ly

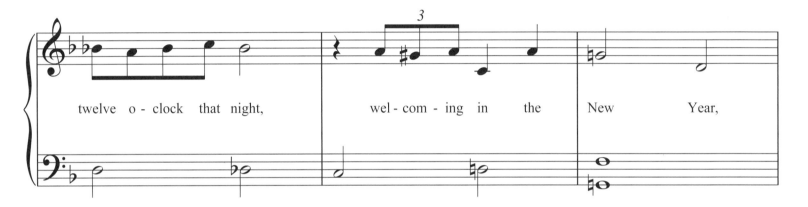

twelve o - clock that night, wel - com - ing in the New Year,

New Year's Eve. May - be I'm cra - zy

to sup - pose I'd ev - er be the one you chose

153

out of the thou - sand   in - vi - ta - tions you'll   re -

ceive.   Ah, but in case I   stand one lit - tle chance,

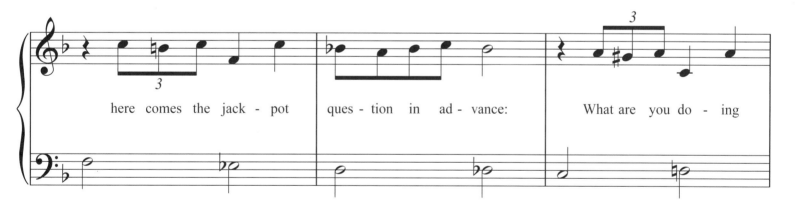

here comes the jack - pot   ques - tion in ad - vance: What are you do - ing

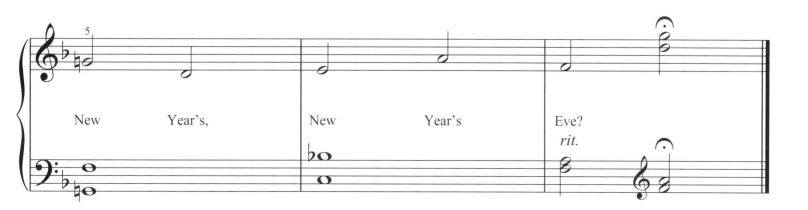

New   Year's,   New   Year's   Eve?

rit.

WHITE CHRISTMAS
from the Motion Picture Irving Berlin's HOLIDAY INN

Words and Music by
IRVING BERLIN

I'm dream - ing of a white

Christ - mas, just like the ones I used to

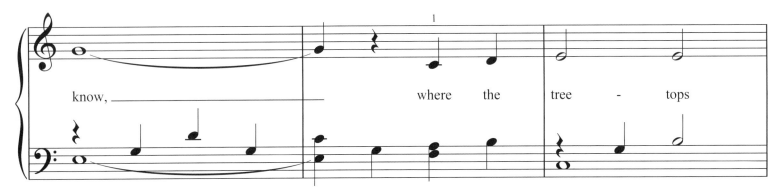

know, where the tree - tops

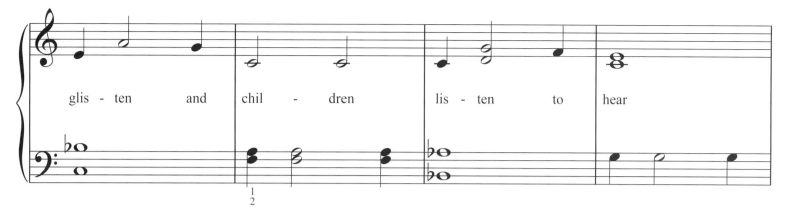

glis - ten   and   chil - dren   lis - ten   to   hear

sleigh - bells   in   the   snow.

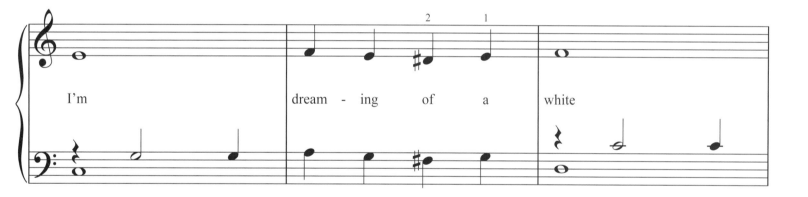

I'm   dream - ing   of   a   white

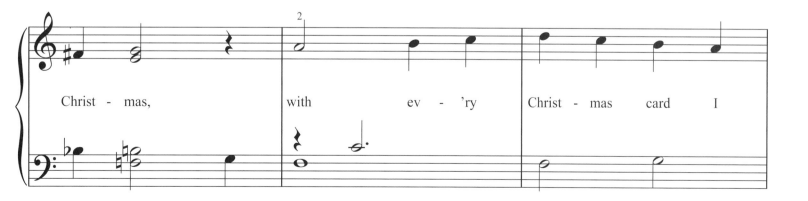

Christ - mas,   with   ev - 'ry   Christ - mas   card   I

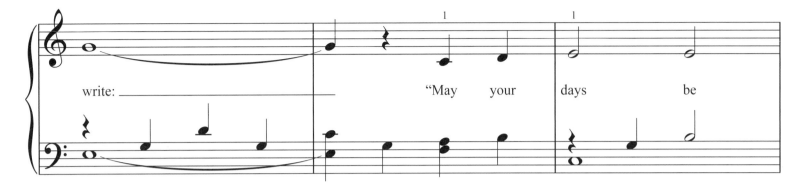

write: _____ "May your days be

mer - ry and bright _____ and may all your

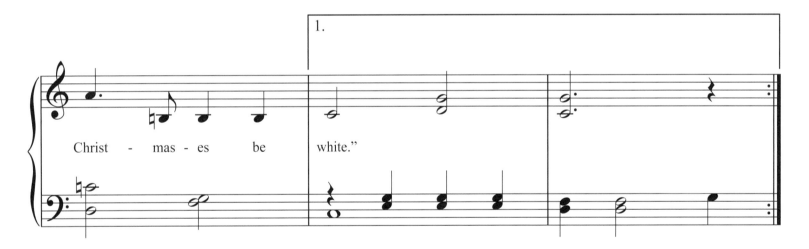

Christ - mas - es be white." | white."

white." rit.

YOU'RE ALL I WANT FOR CHRISTMAS

Words and Music by GLEN MOORE
and SEGER ELLIS

Moderately

When San-ta comes a-round at Christ-mas time and

leaves a lot of cheer at ev-'ry door, if he would on-ly grant the

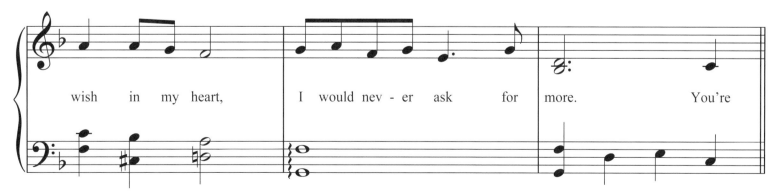

wish in my heart, I would nev-er ask for more. You're

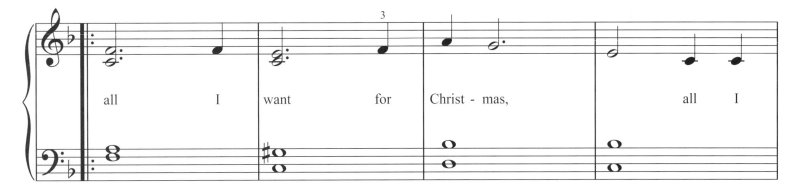

all   I   want   for   Christ - mas,   all   I

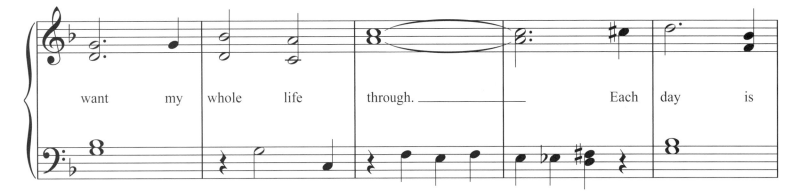

want   my   whole   life   through. _____   Each   day   is

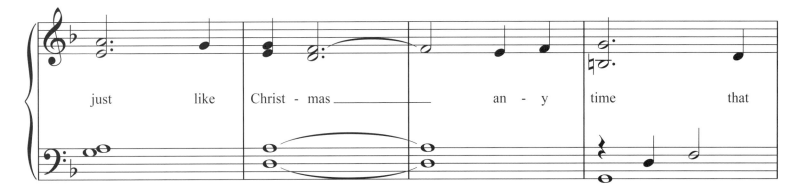

just   like   Christ - mas _____   an - y   time   that

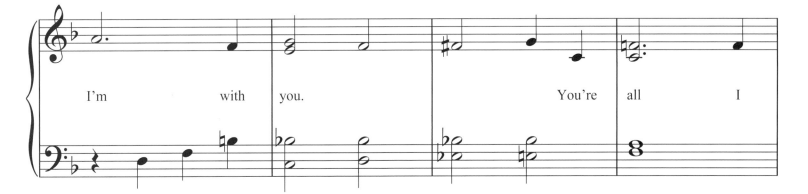

I'm   with   you.   You're   all   I

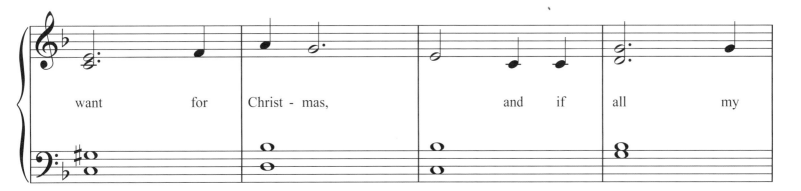

want   for   Christ - mas,   and   if   all   my

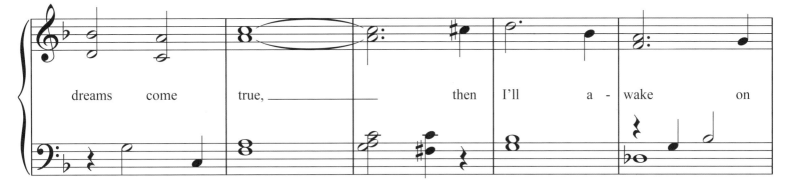

dreams   come   true,   then   I'll   a - wake   on

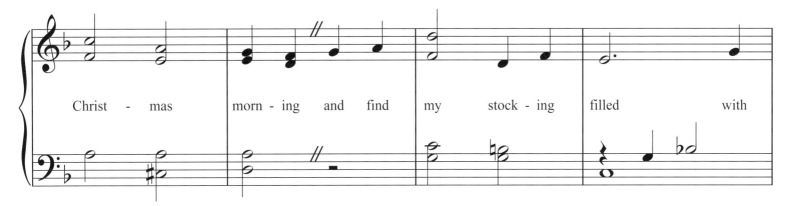

Christ - mas   morn - ing   and   find   my   stock - ing   filled   with

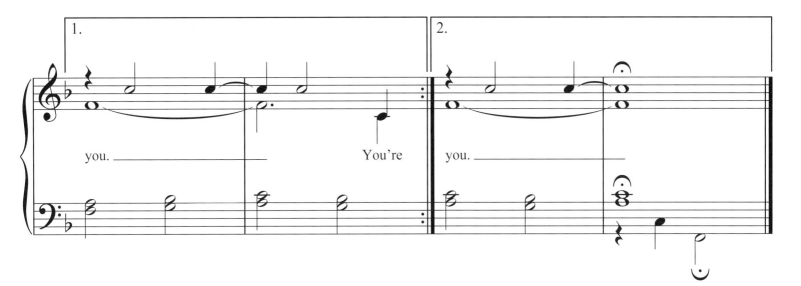

you.   You're   you.

WONDERFUL CHRISTMASTIME

Words and Music by
PAUL McCARTNEY

The mood is right,
The par - ty's on,
The word is out

the spir - it's up,
the feel - ing's here
a - bout the town,

we're here to - night
that on - ly comes
to lift a glass,

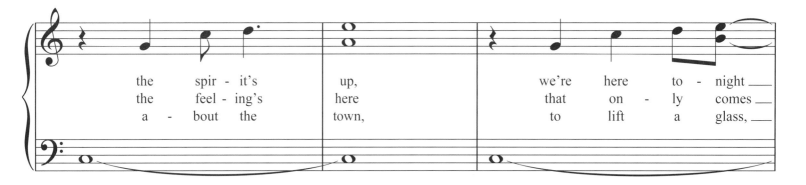

and that's e - nough.
this time of year.
oh, don't look down.

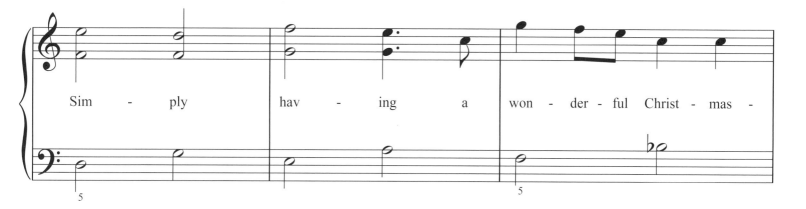

Sim - ply   hav - ing   a   won - der - ful   Christ - mas -

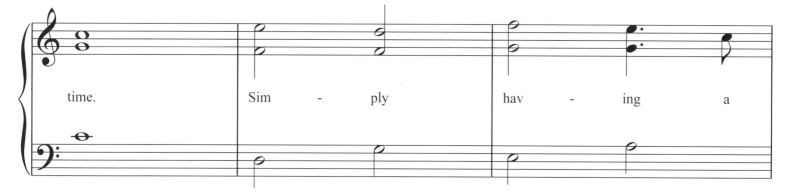

time.   Sim - ply   hav - ing   a

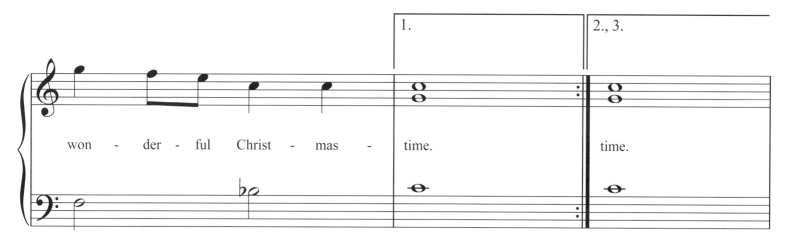

won - der - ful   Christ - mas -   time.   time.

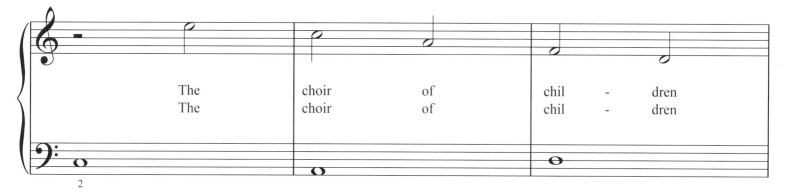

The   choir   of   chil - dren
The   choir   of   chil - dren

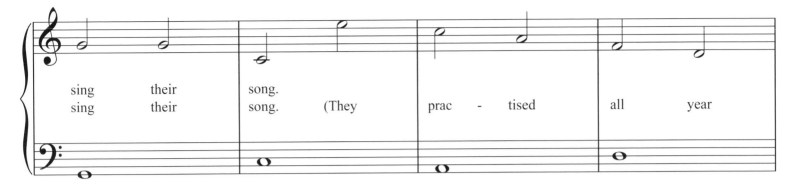

sing   their   song.
sing   their   song.   (They   prac - tised   all   year

To Coda $\oplus$

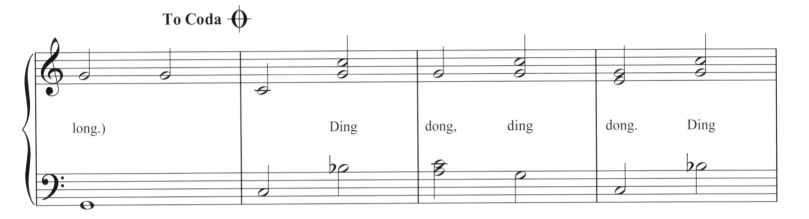

long.)   Ding   dong,   ding   dong.   Ding

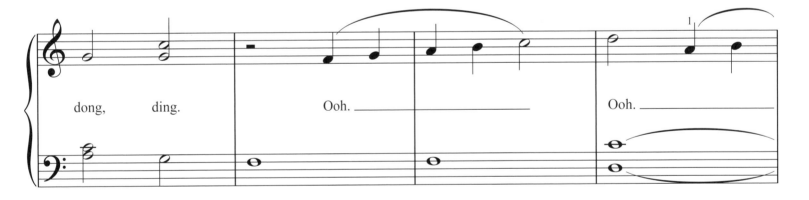

dong,   ding.   Ooh.   Ooh.

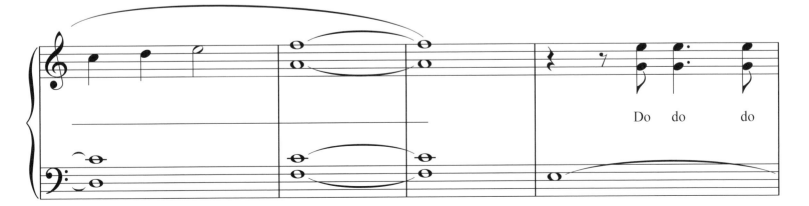

Do   do   do

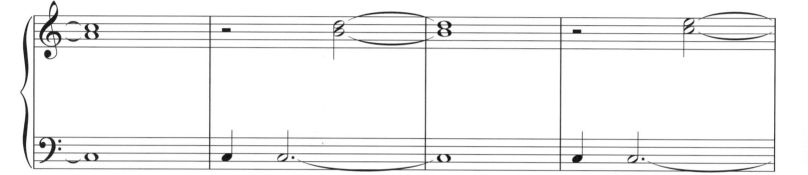

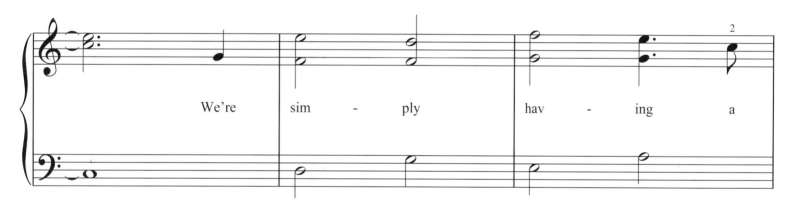

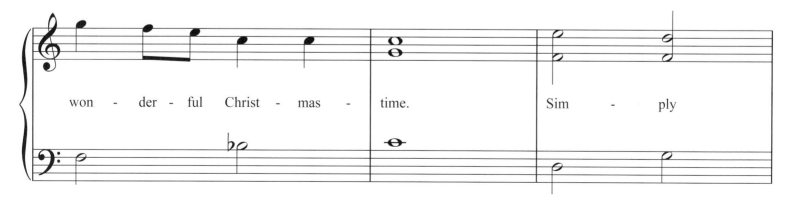

do   do   do   do.

We're   sim -   ply   hav -   ing   a

2

won - der - ful Christ - mas -   time.   Sim -   ply

D.S. al Coda

hav - ing a won - der - ful Christ - mas - time.

CODA

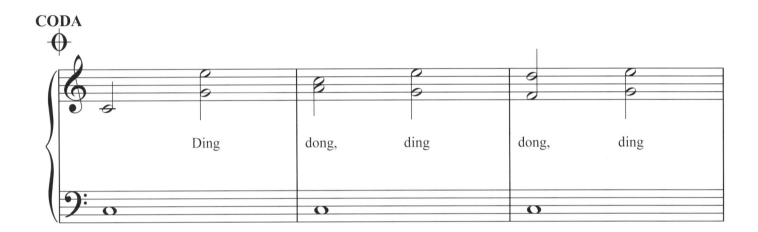

Ding dong, ding dong, ding

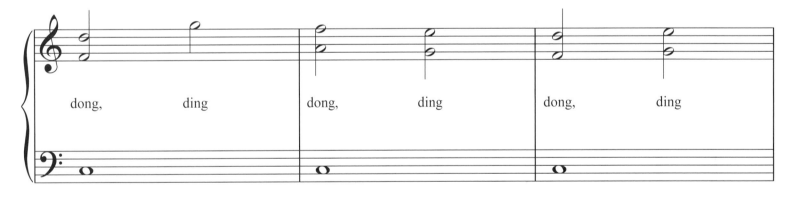

dong, ding dong, ding dong, ding

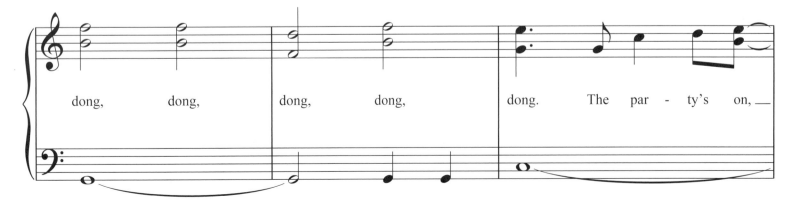

dong, dong, dong, dong, dong. The par - ty's on, ___

the spir - it's up,

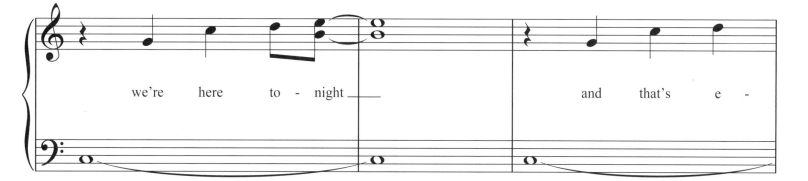

we're here to - night ___ and that's e -

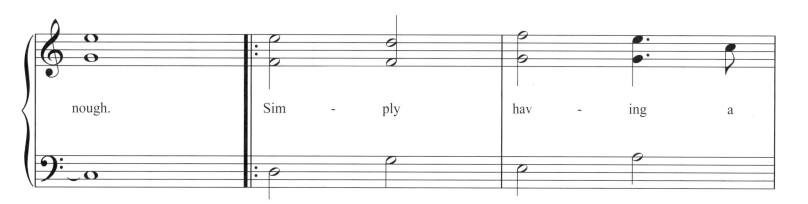

nough. Sim - ply hav - ing a

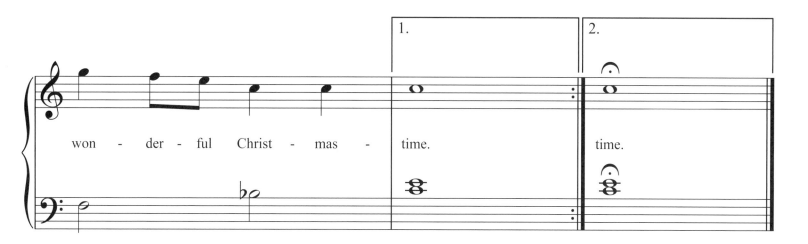

won - der - ful Christ - mas - time. time.

WINTER WONDERLAND

Words by DICK SMITH
Music by FELIX BERNARD

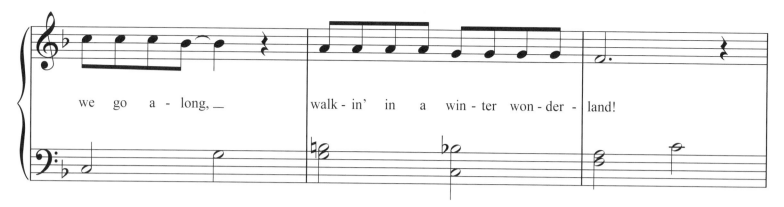

we go a - long, ___ walk - in' in a win - ter won - der - land!

In the mead - ow we can build a snow - man, then pre - tend that he is Par - son
In the mead - ow we can build a snow - man, and pre - tend that he's a cir - cus

Brown.
clown.

He'll say, "Are you mar - ried?" We'll say, "No, man! But
We'll have lots of fun with Mis - ter Snow - man un -

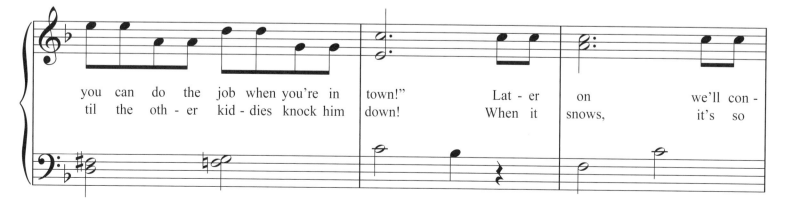

you can do the job when you're in town!" Lat - er on we'll con -
til the oth - er kid - dies knock him down! When it snows, it's so

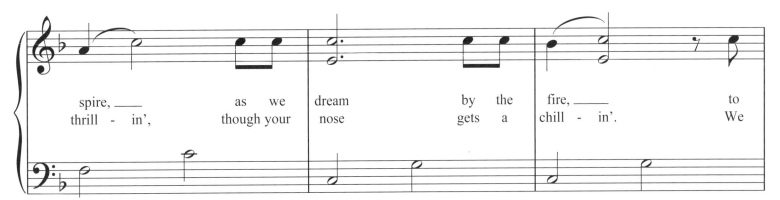

spire, _____ as we dream by the fire, _____ to
thrill - in', though your nose gets a chill - in'. We

face un - a - fraid _____ the plans that we made _____ walk - in' in a win - ter won - der -
frol - ic and play _____ the Es - ki - mo way, _____ walk - in' in a win - ter won - der -

1.
land! Sleigh-bells

2.
land, walk - in' in a win - ter won - der -

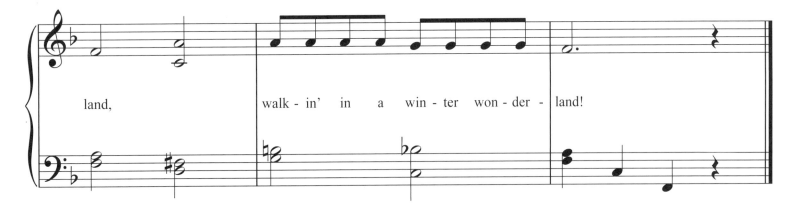

land, walk - in' in a win - ter won - der - land!